W0081913

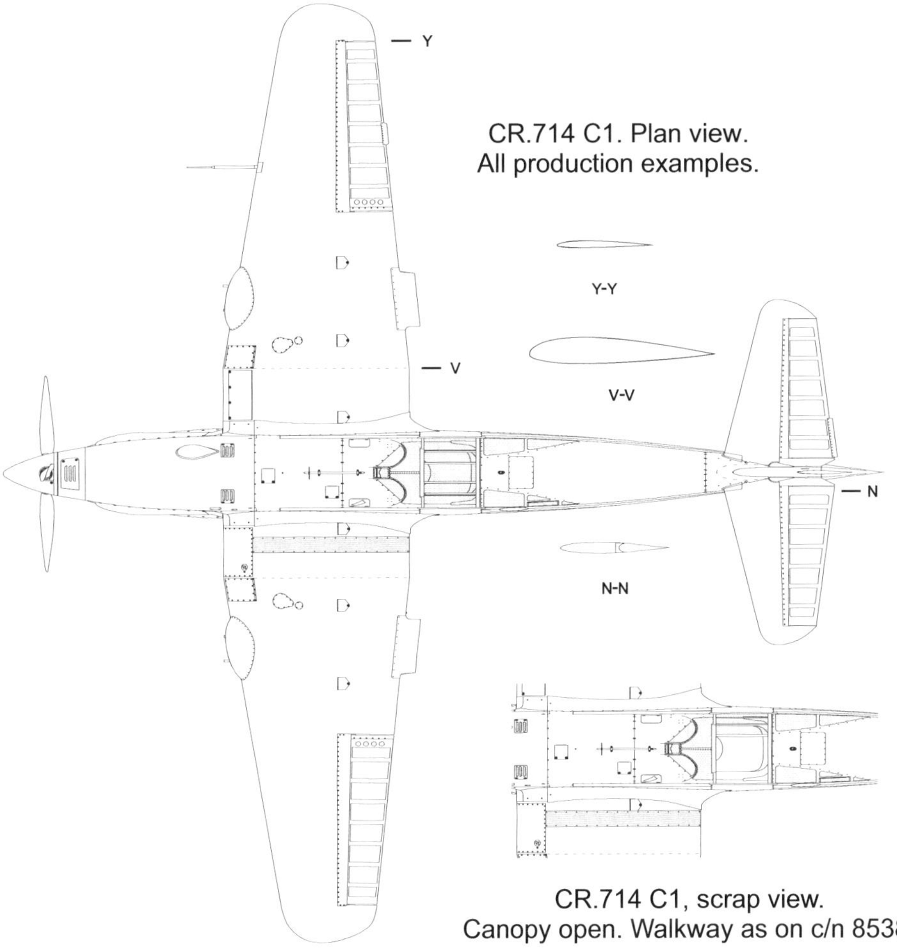

CR.714 C1. Plan view.
All production examples.

Y-Y

V-V

N-N

CR.714 C1, scrap view.
Canopy open. Walkway as on c/n 8538.

CR.714 C
underca
Fuselage

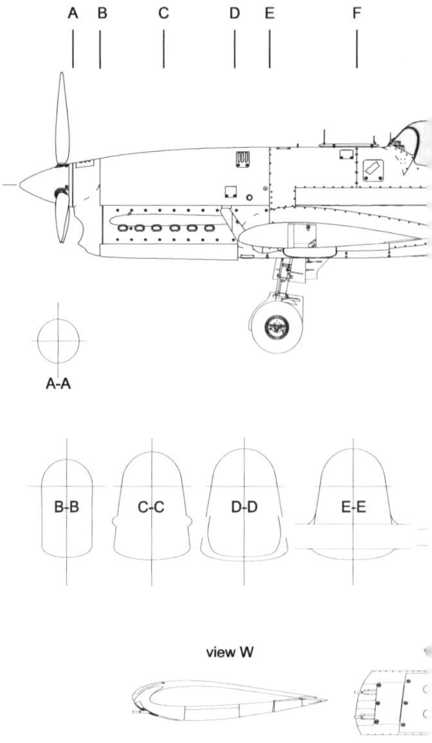

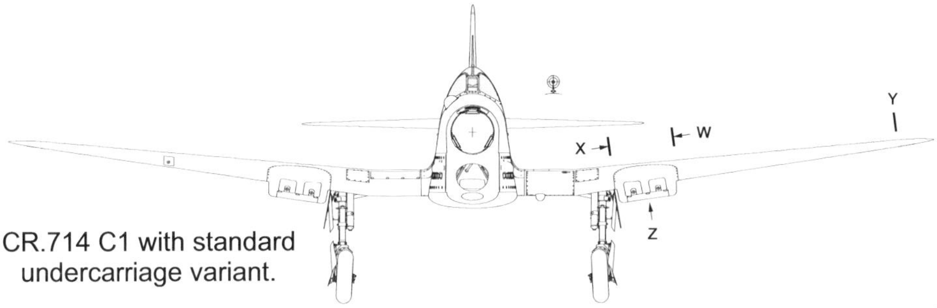

A-A

B-B   C-C   D-D   E-E

view W

CR.714 C1 with standard
undercarriage variant.

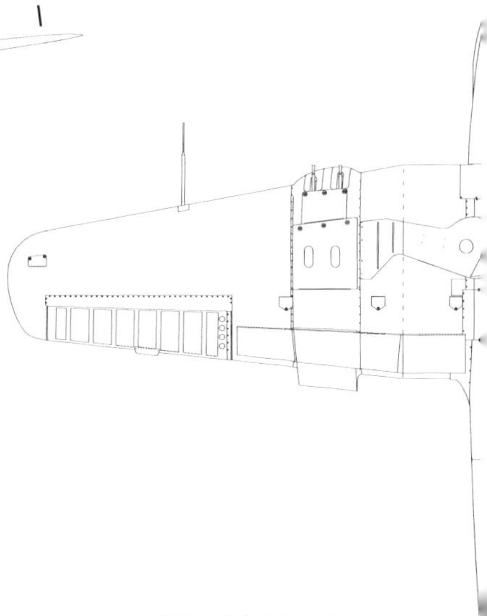

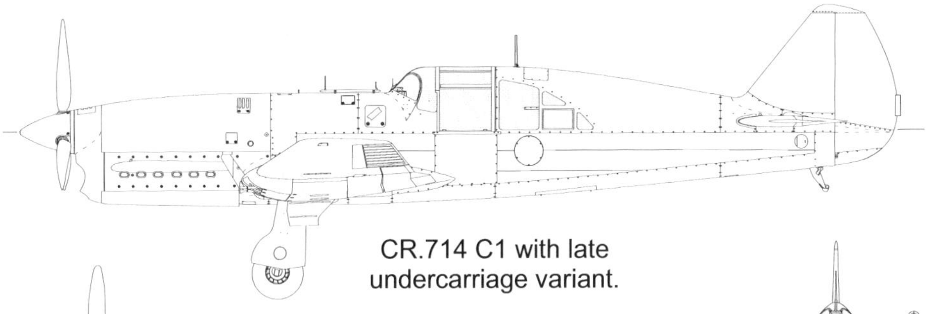

CR.714 C1 with late
undercarriage variant.

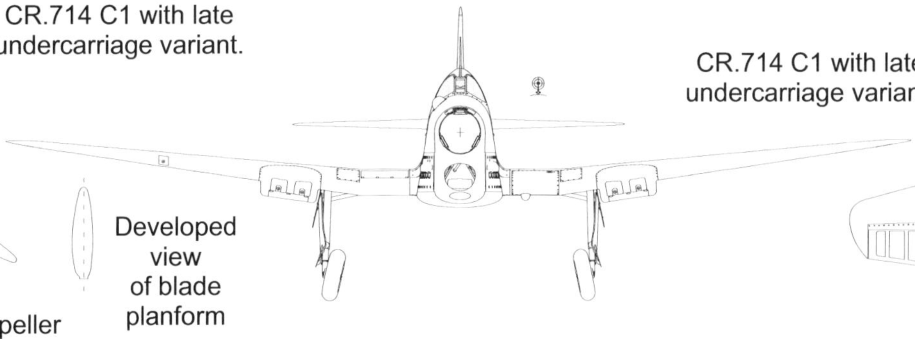

CR.714 C1 with late
undercarriage variant.

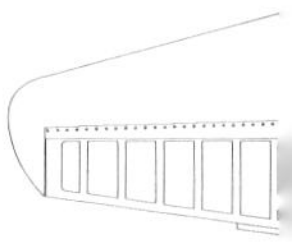

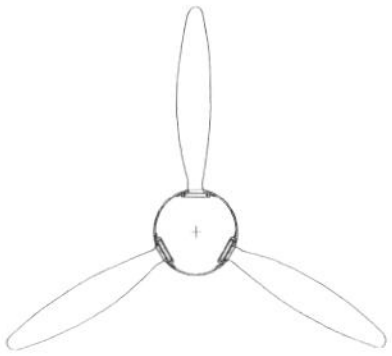

Fine pitch

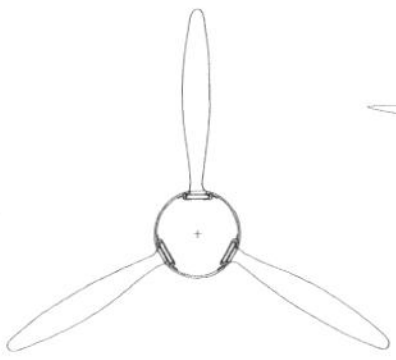

Coarse pitch

Ratier 1644MV propeller

Developed
view
of blade
planform

© Franciszek Strzelczyk
 & Tomasz Bobkowski

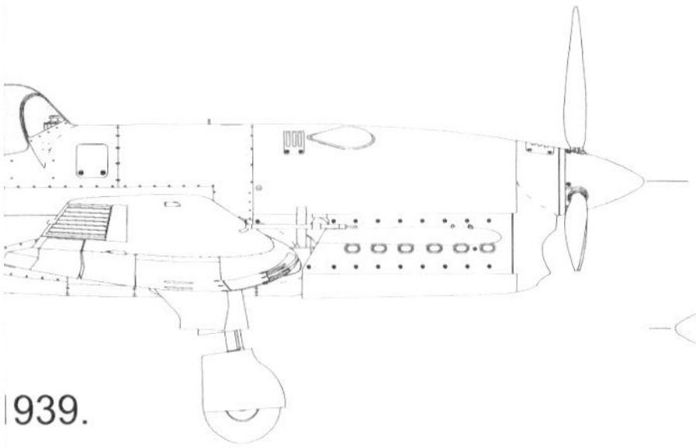

939.

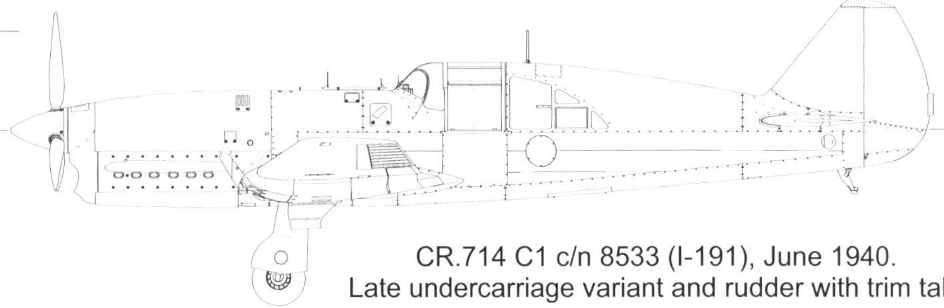

CR.714 C1 c/n 8533 (I-191), June 1940.
Late undercarriage variant and rudder with trim tab.

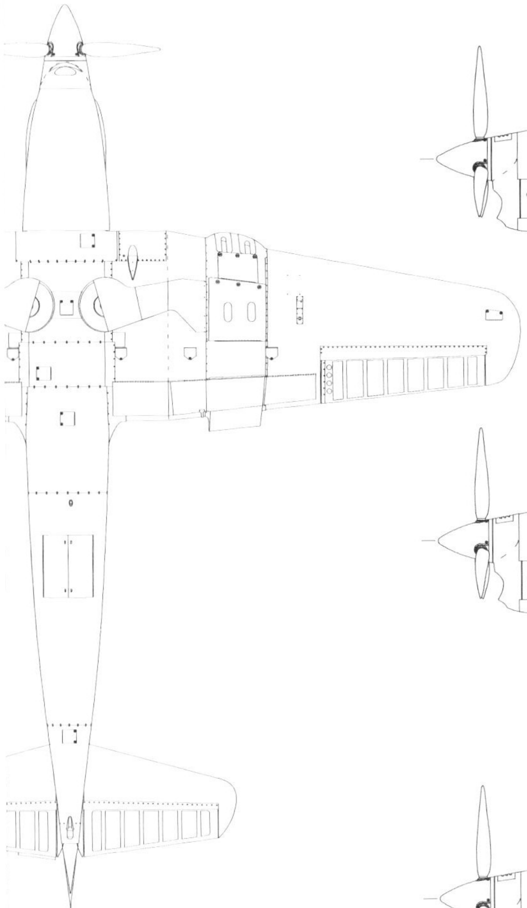

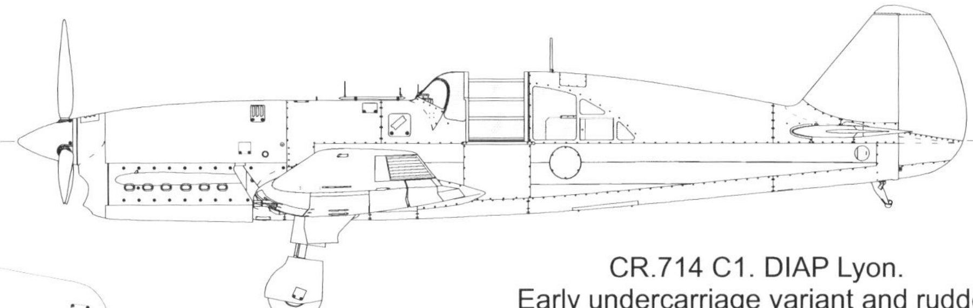

CR.714 C1. DIAP Lyon.
Early undercarriage variant and rudder
without trim tab. Canopy shown open.

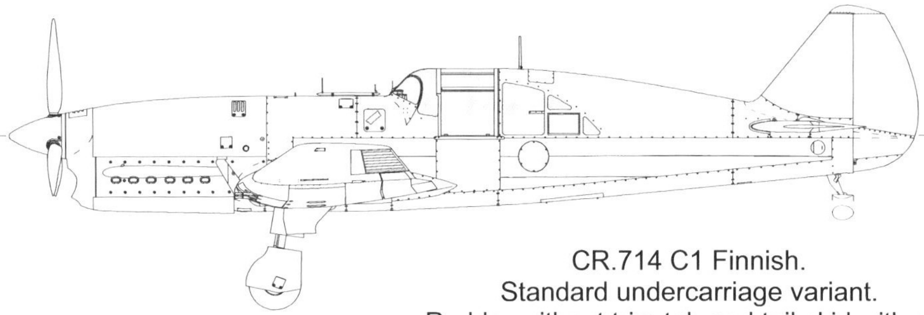

CR.714 C1 Finnish.
Standard undercarriage variant.
Rudder without trim tab and tail skid with ski.

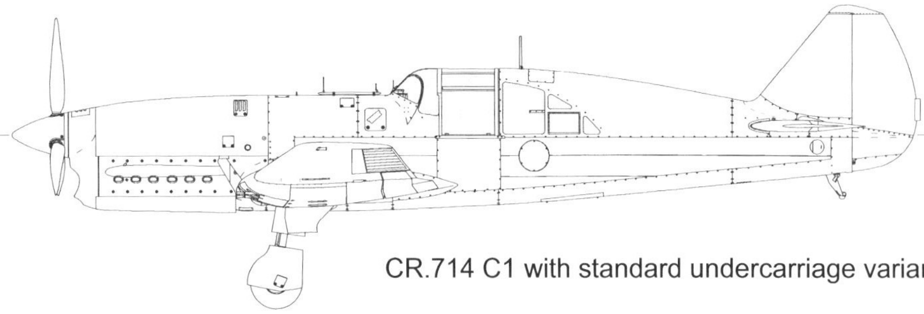

CR.714 C1 with standard undercarriage variant.

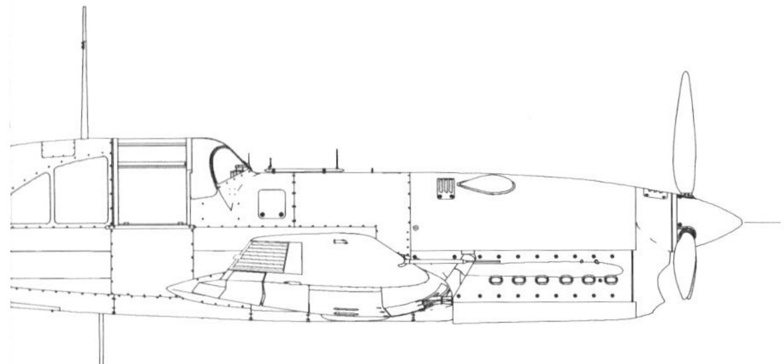

...configuration, antennas fully extended.
...production examples.

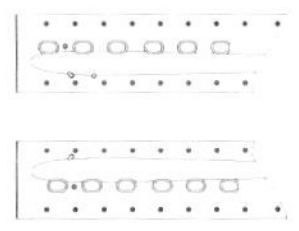

Left and right engine covers.
Note different location of openings for exhaust pipes.
All examples.

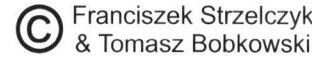

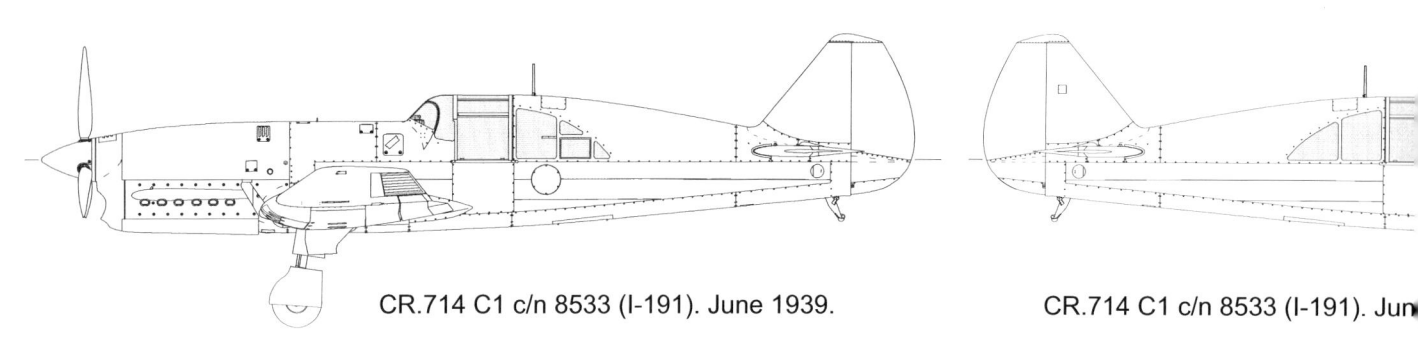

CR.714 C1 c/n 8533 (I-191). June 1939.

CR.714 C1 c/n 8533 (I-191). Jun

CR.714 C1 c/n 8533 (I-191). June 1939.

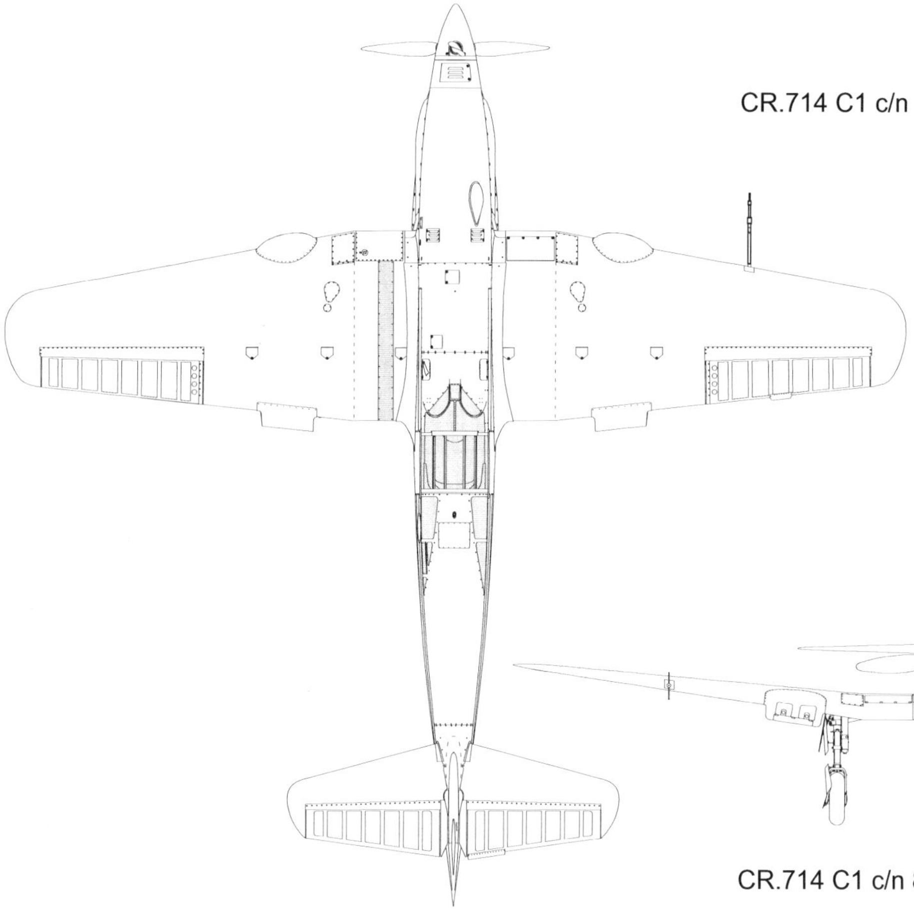

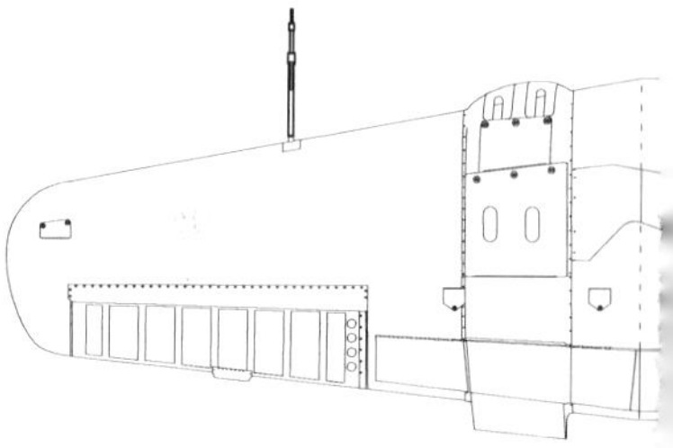

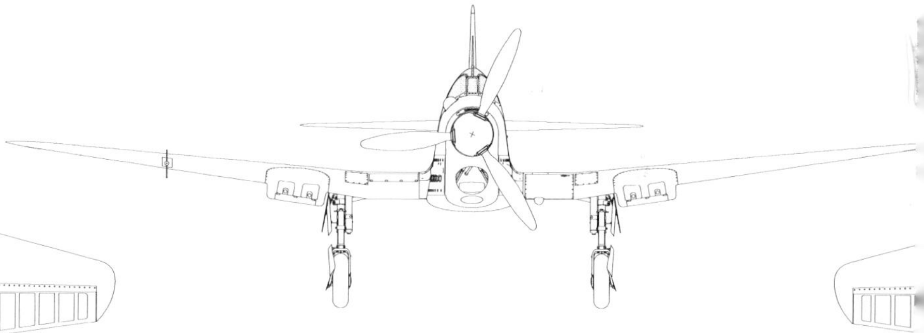

CR.714 C1 c/n 8533 (I-191). June 1939.

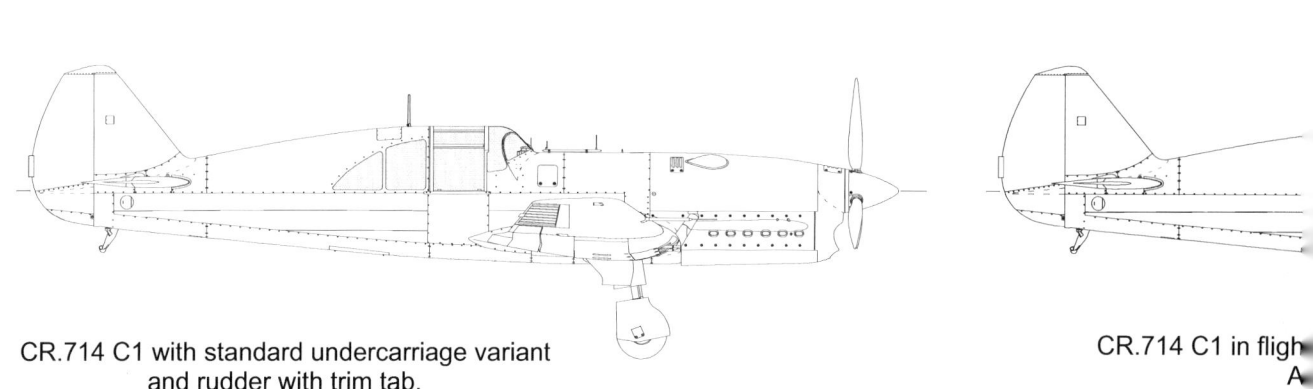

CR.714 C1 with standard undercarriage variant
and rudder with trim tab.

CR.714 C1 in fligh
A

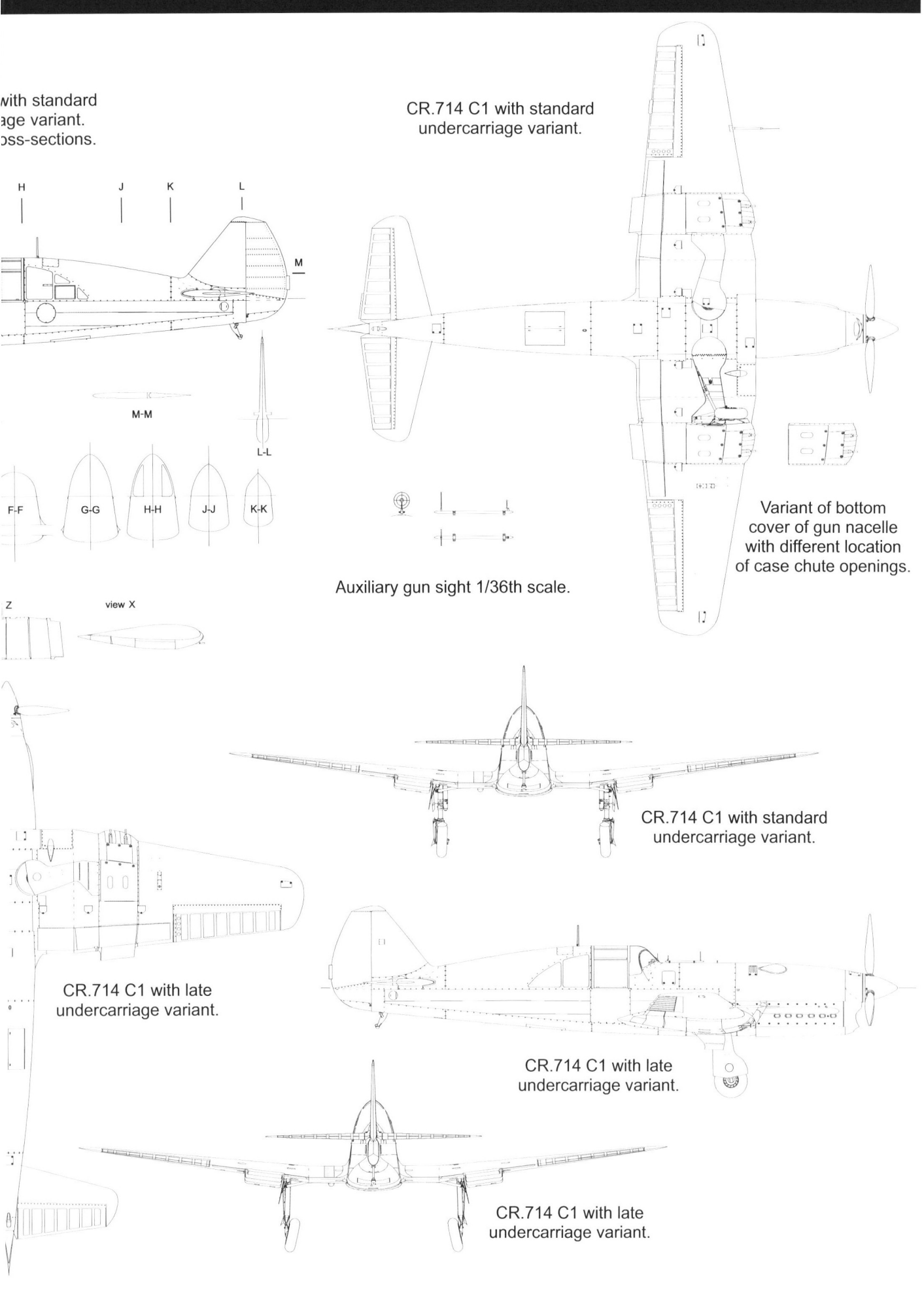

with standard
age variant.
oss-sections.

H   J   K   L

M

M-M

L-L

F-F   G-G   H-H   J-J   K-K

Z   view X

CR.714 C1 with standard
undercarriage variant.

Variant of bottom
cover of gun nacelle
with different location
of case chute openings.

Auxiliary gun sight 1/36th scale.

CR.714 C1 with standard
undercarriage variant.

CR.714 C1 with late
undercarriage variant.

CR.714 C1 with late
undercarriage variant.

CR.714 C1 with late
undercarriage variant.

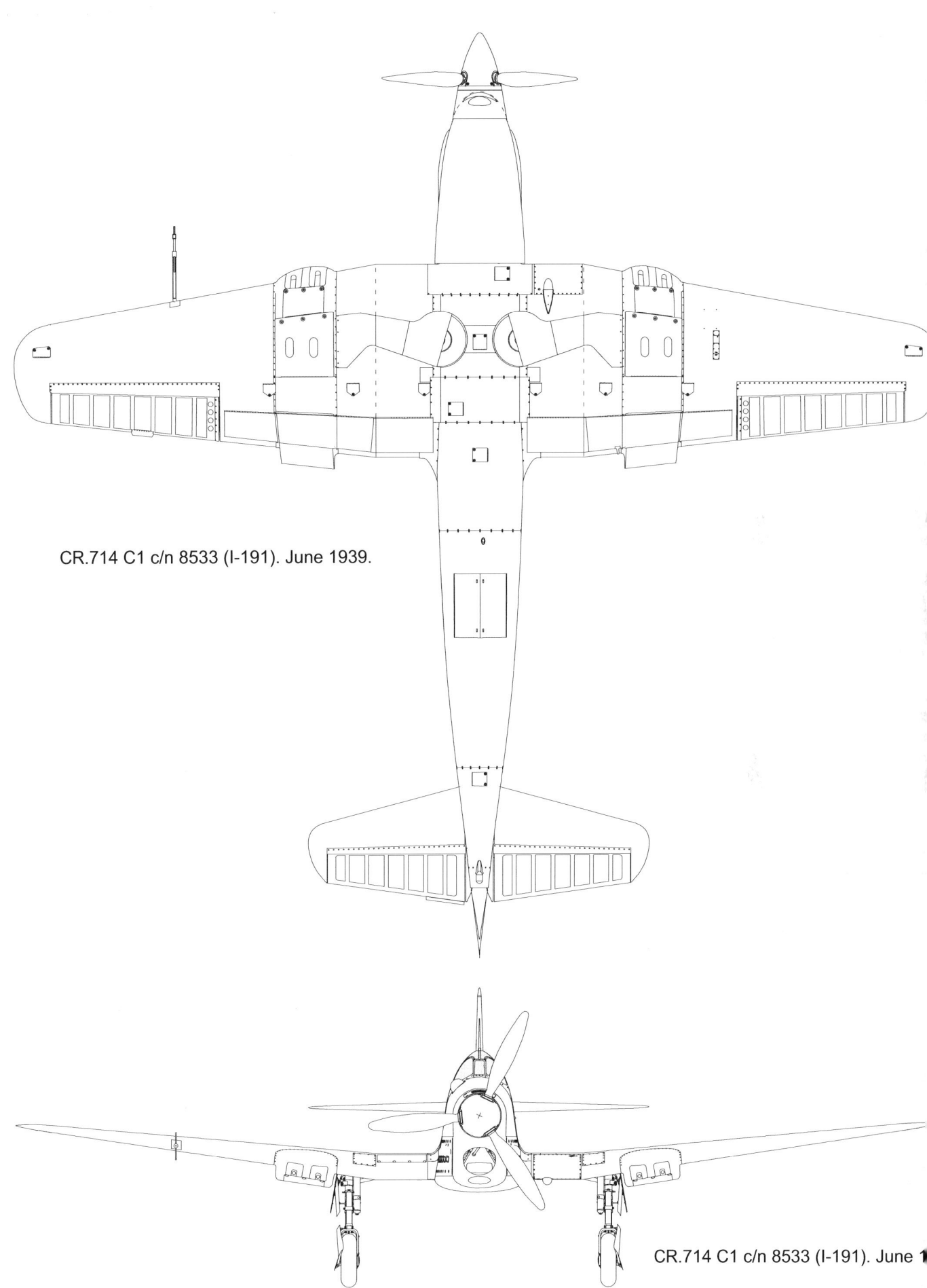

CR.714 C1 c/n 8533 (I-191). June 1939.

CR.714 C1 c/n 8533 (I-191). June 1

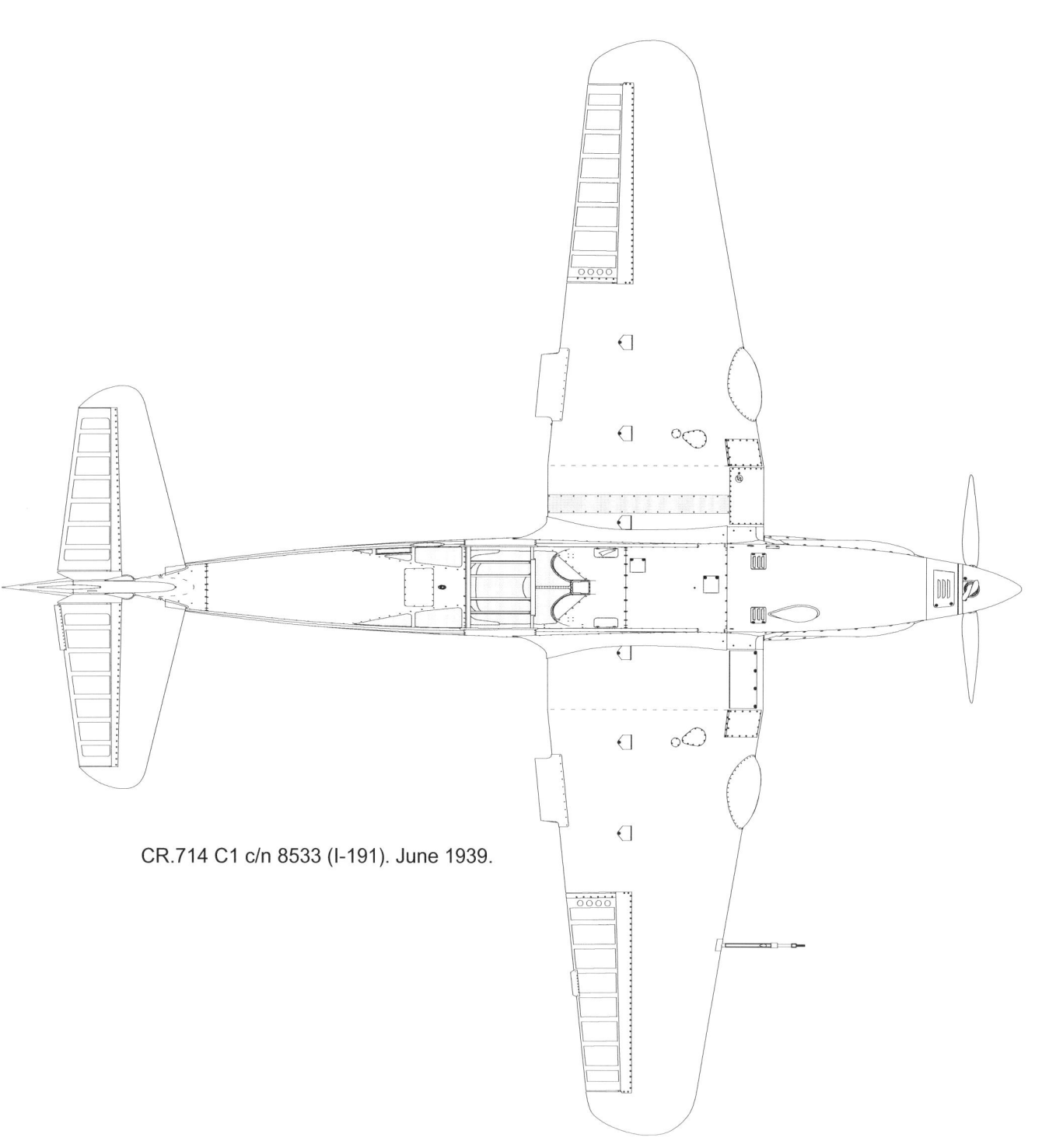

CR.714 C1 c/n 8533 (I-191). June 1939.

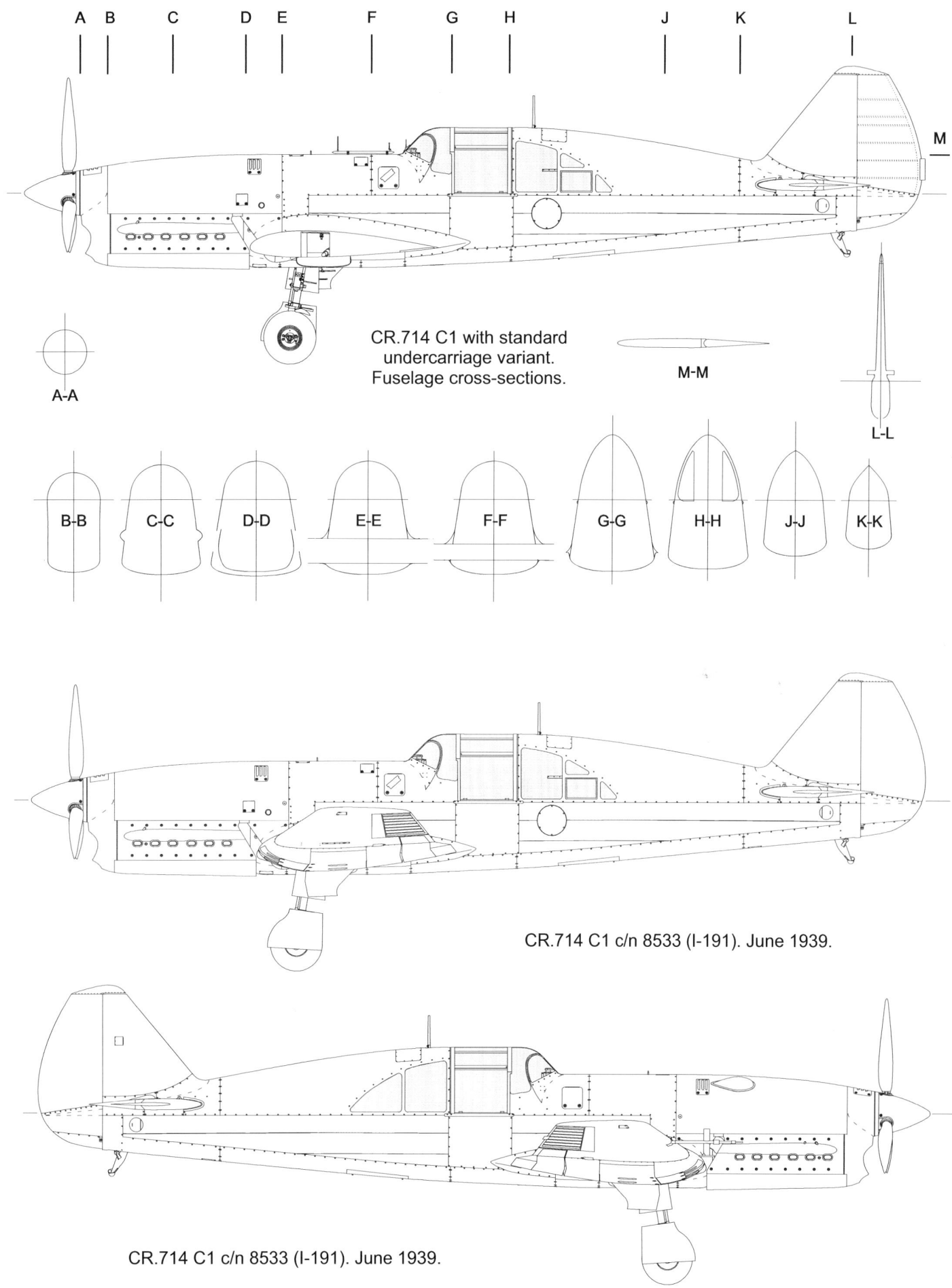

A B   C   D E   F   G   H   J   K   L

M

A-A

M-M

L-L

CR.714 C1 with standard
undercarriage variant.
Fuselage cross-sections.

B-B   C-C   D-D   E-E   F-F   G-G   H-H   J-J   K-K

CR.714 C1 c/n 8533 (I-191). June 1939.

CR.714 C1 c/n 8533 (I-191). June 1939.

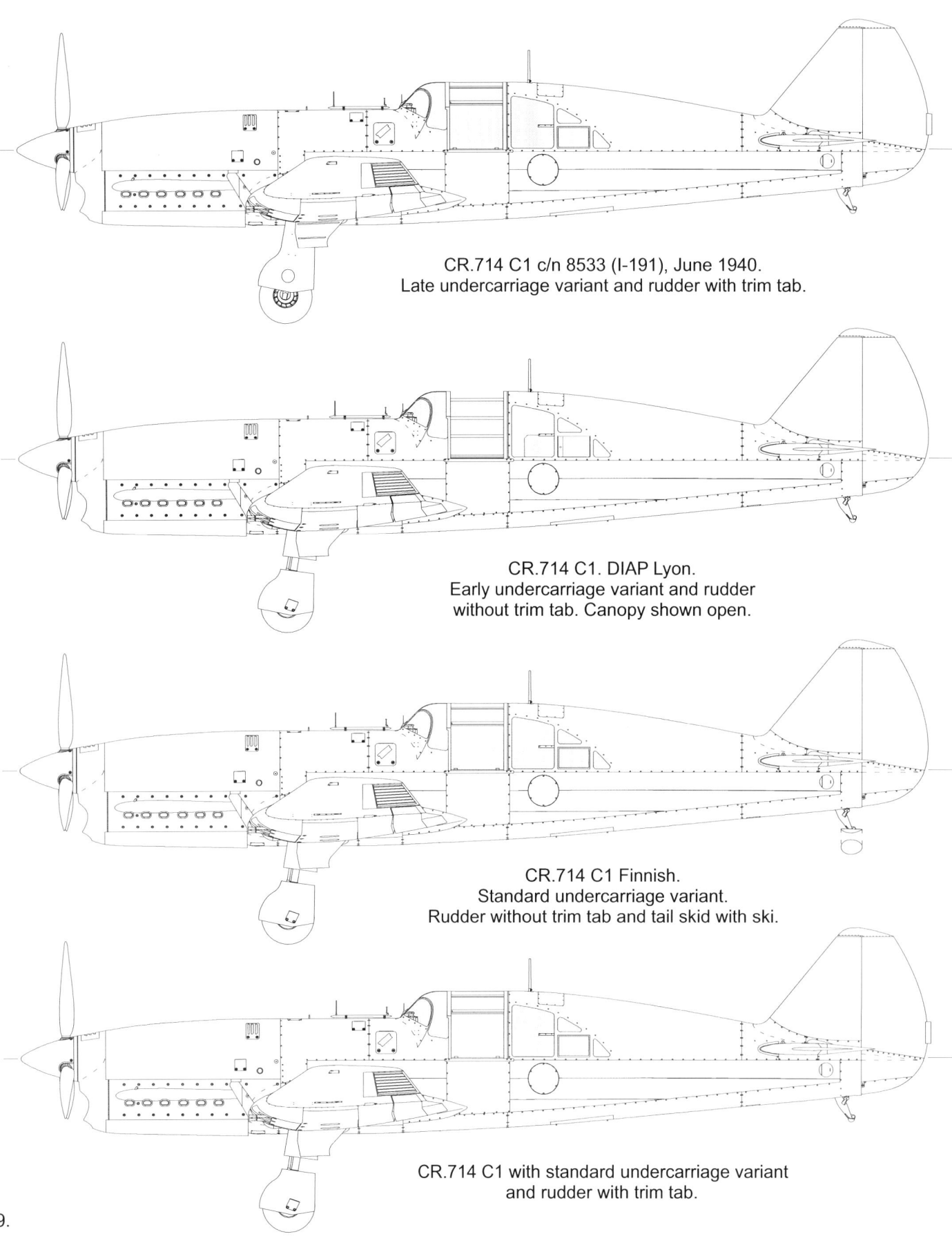

CR.714 C1 c/n 8533 (I-191), June 1940.
Late undercarriage variant and rudder with trim tab.

CR.714 C1. DIAP Lyon.
Early undercarriage variant and rudder
without trim tab. Canopy shown open.

CR.714 C1 Finnish.
Standard undercarriage variant.
Rudder without trim tab and tail skid with ski.

CR.714 C1 with standard undercarriage variant
and rudder with trim tab.

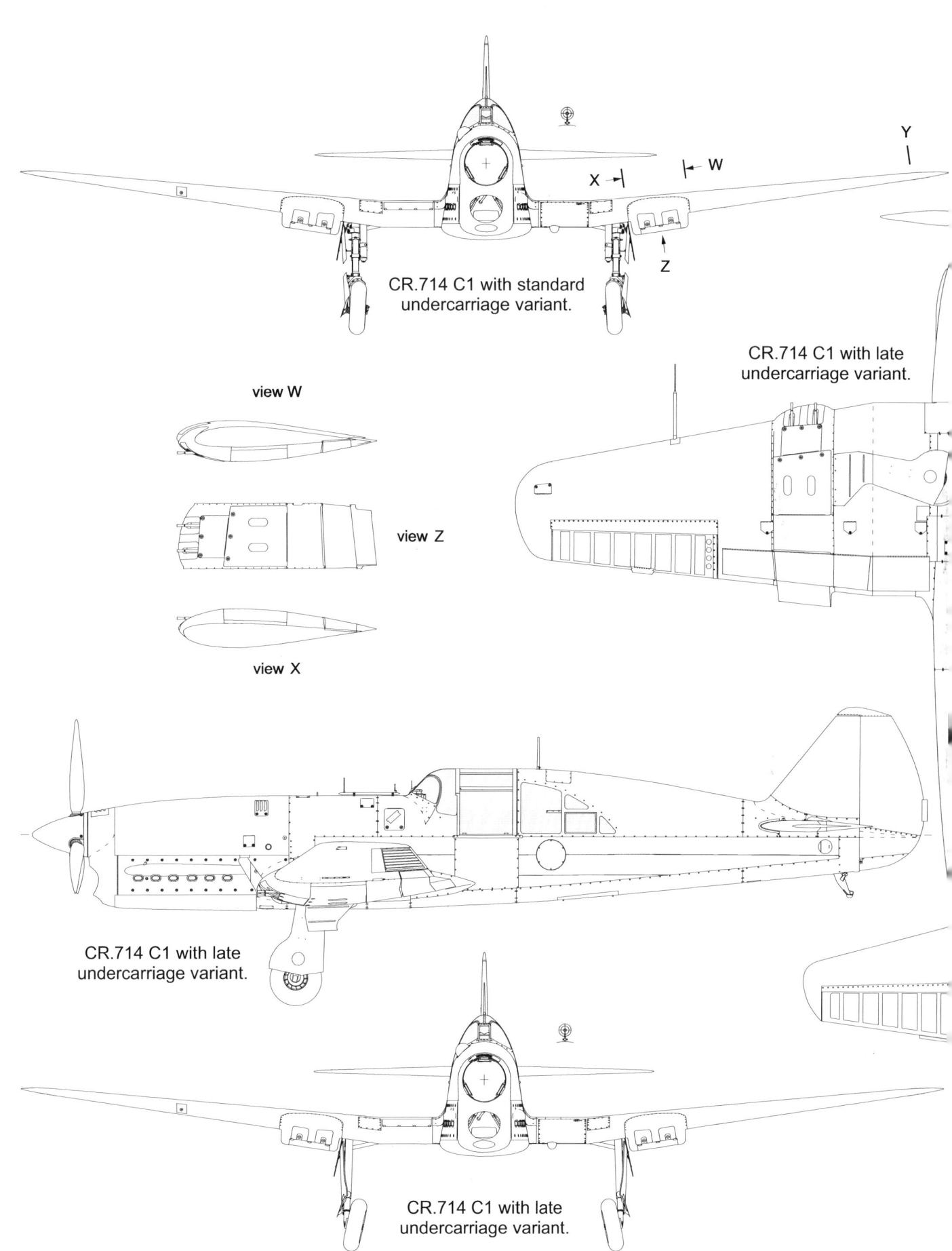

CR.714 C1 with standard undercarriage variant.

CR.714 C1 with late undercarriage variant.

view W

view Z

view X

CR.714 C1 with late undercarriage variant.

CR.714 C1 with late undercarriage variant.

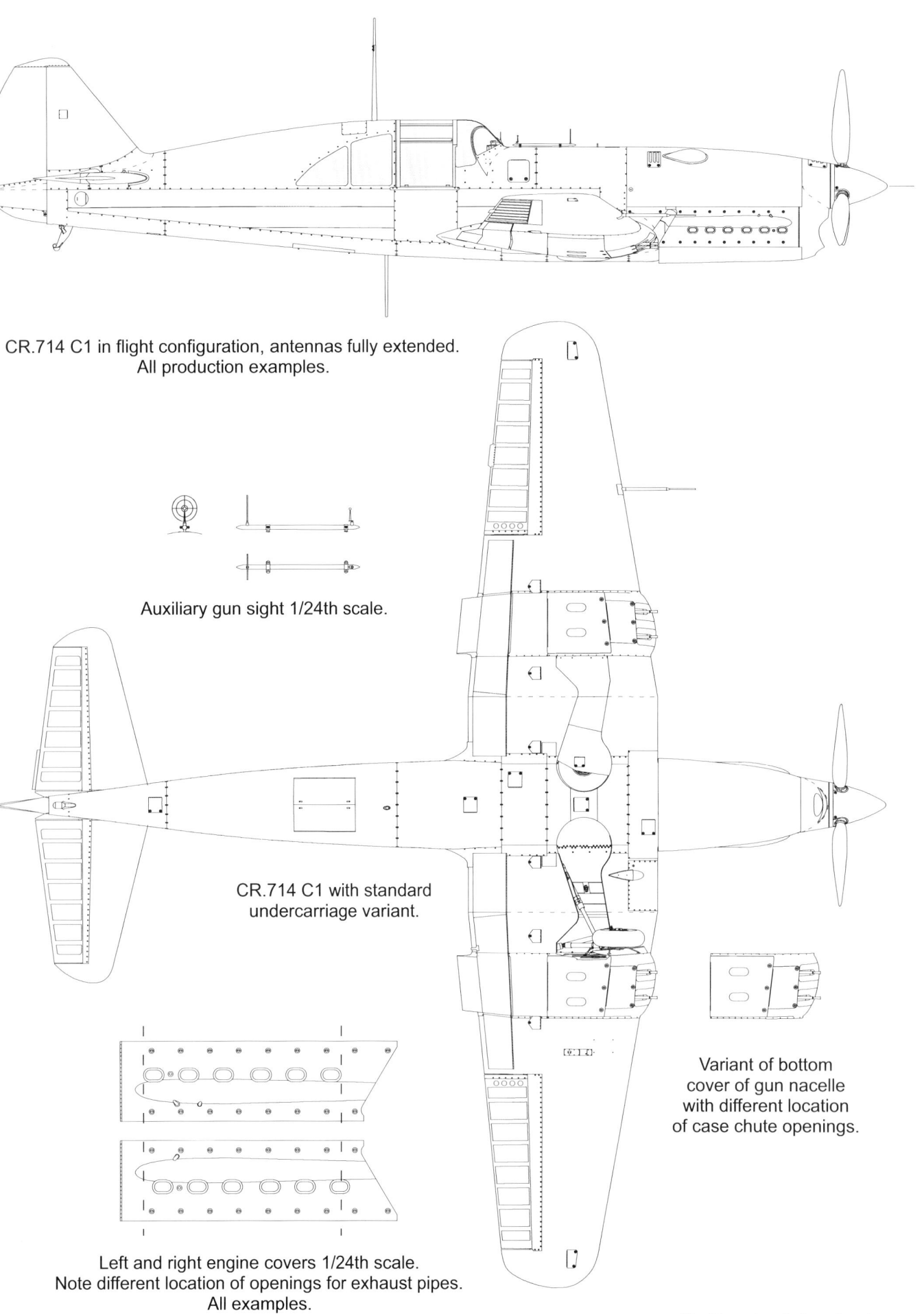

CR.714 C1 in flight configuration, antennas fully extended.
All production examples.

Auxiliary gun sight 1/24th scale.

CR.714 C1 with standard
undercarriage variant.

Variant of bottom
cover of gun nacelle
with different location
of case chute openings.

Left and right engine covers 1/24th scale.
Note different location of openings for exhaust pipes.
All examples.

© Franciszek Strzelczyk
& Tomasz Bobkowski

5

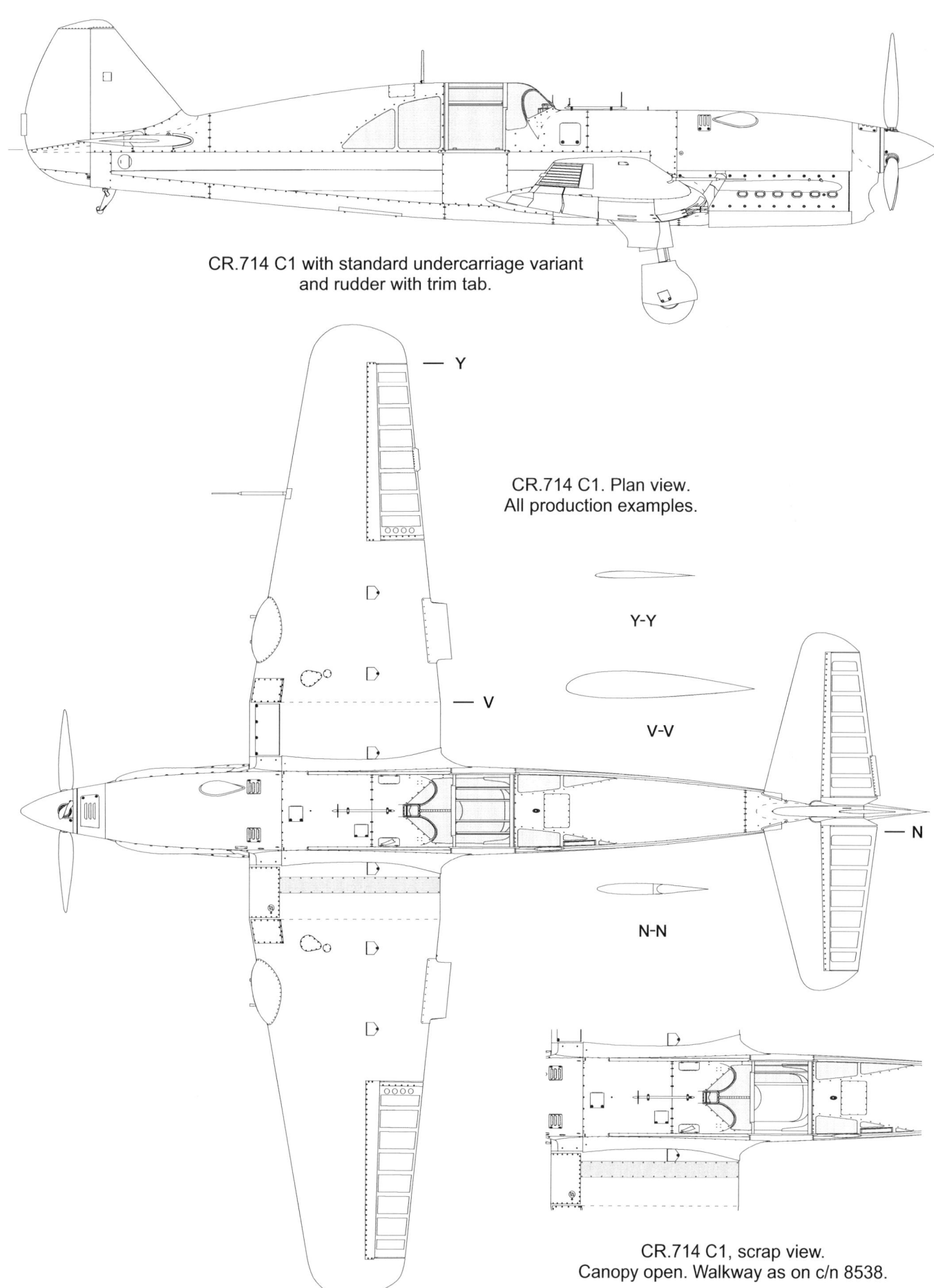

CR.714 C1 with standard undercarriage variant
and rudder with trim tab.

CR.714 C1. Plan view.
All production examples.

Y-Y

V-V

N-N

CR.714 C1, scrap view.
Canopy open. Walkway as on c/n 8538.

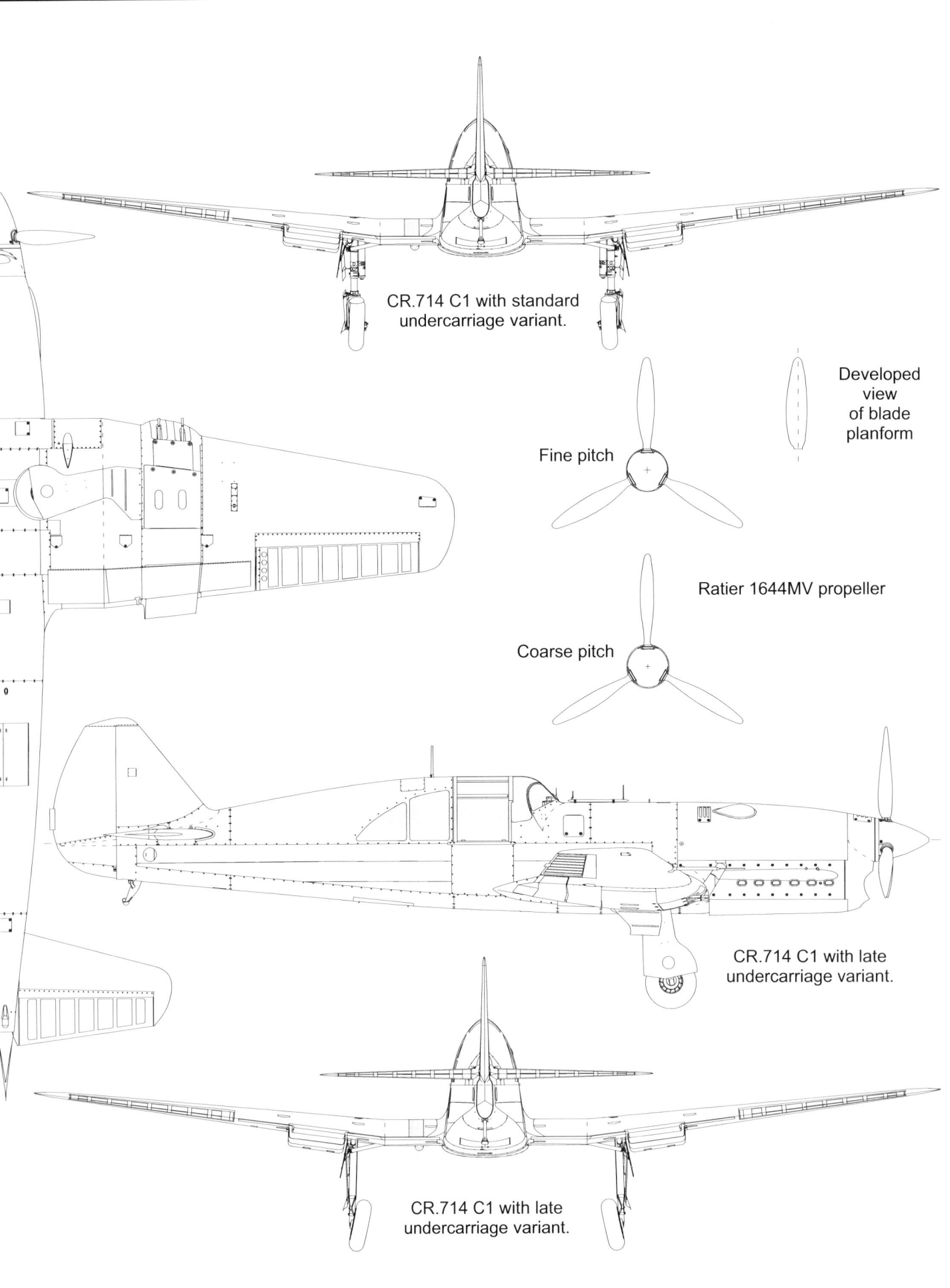

CR.714 C1 with standard
undercarriage variant.

Developed
view
of blade
planform

Fine pitch

Ratier 1644MV propeller

Coarse pitch

CR.714 C1 with late
undercarriage variant.

CR.714 C1 with late
undercarriage variant.

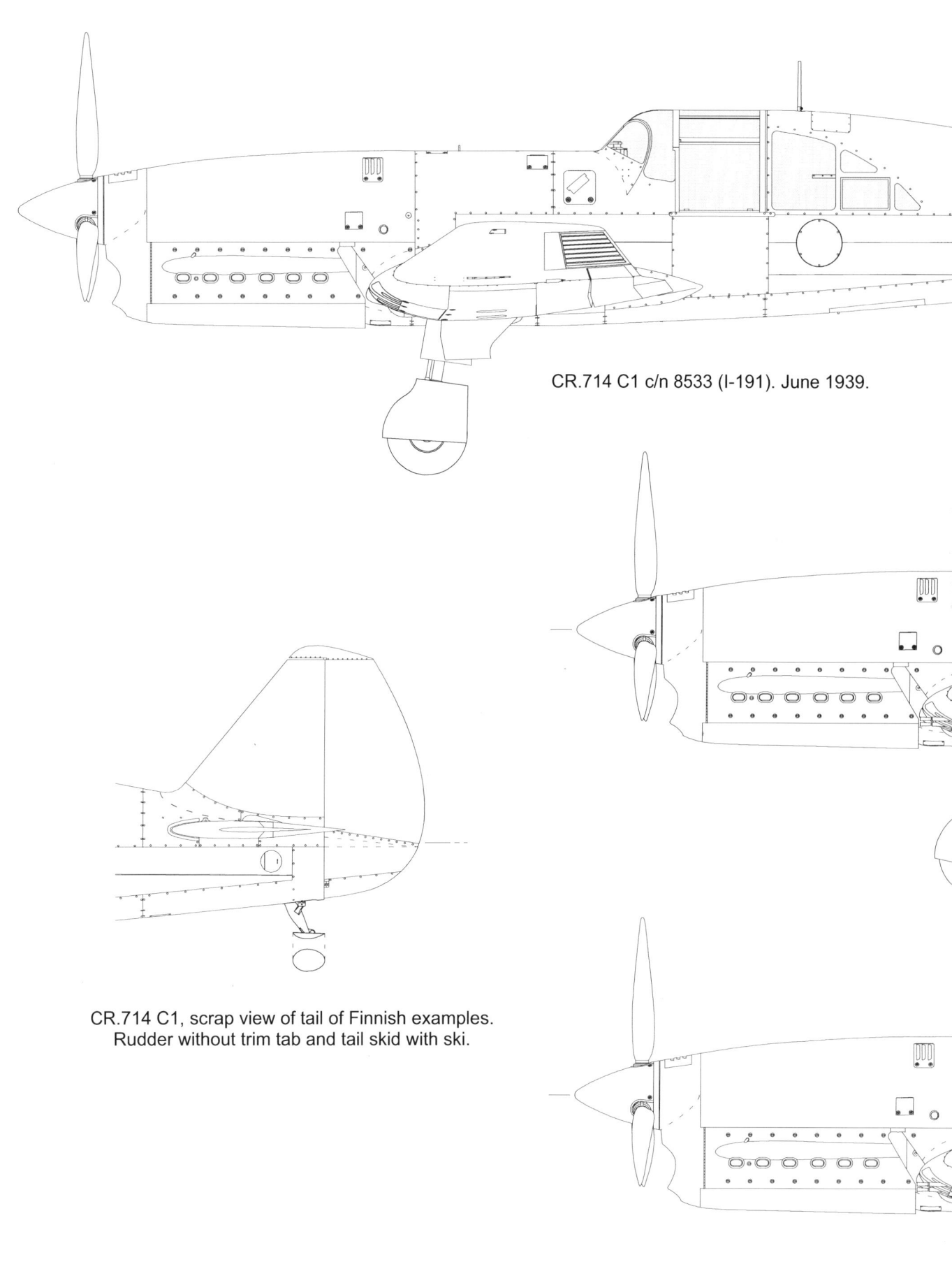

CR.714 C1 c/n 8533 (I-191). June 1939.

CR.714 C1, scrap view of tail of Finnish examples.
Rudder without trim tab and tail skid with ski.

J   K   L

M

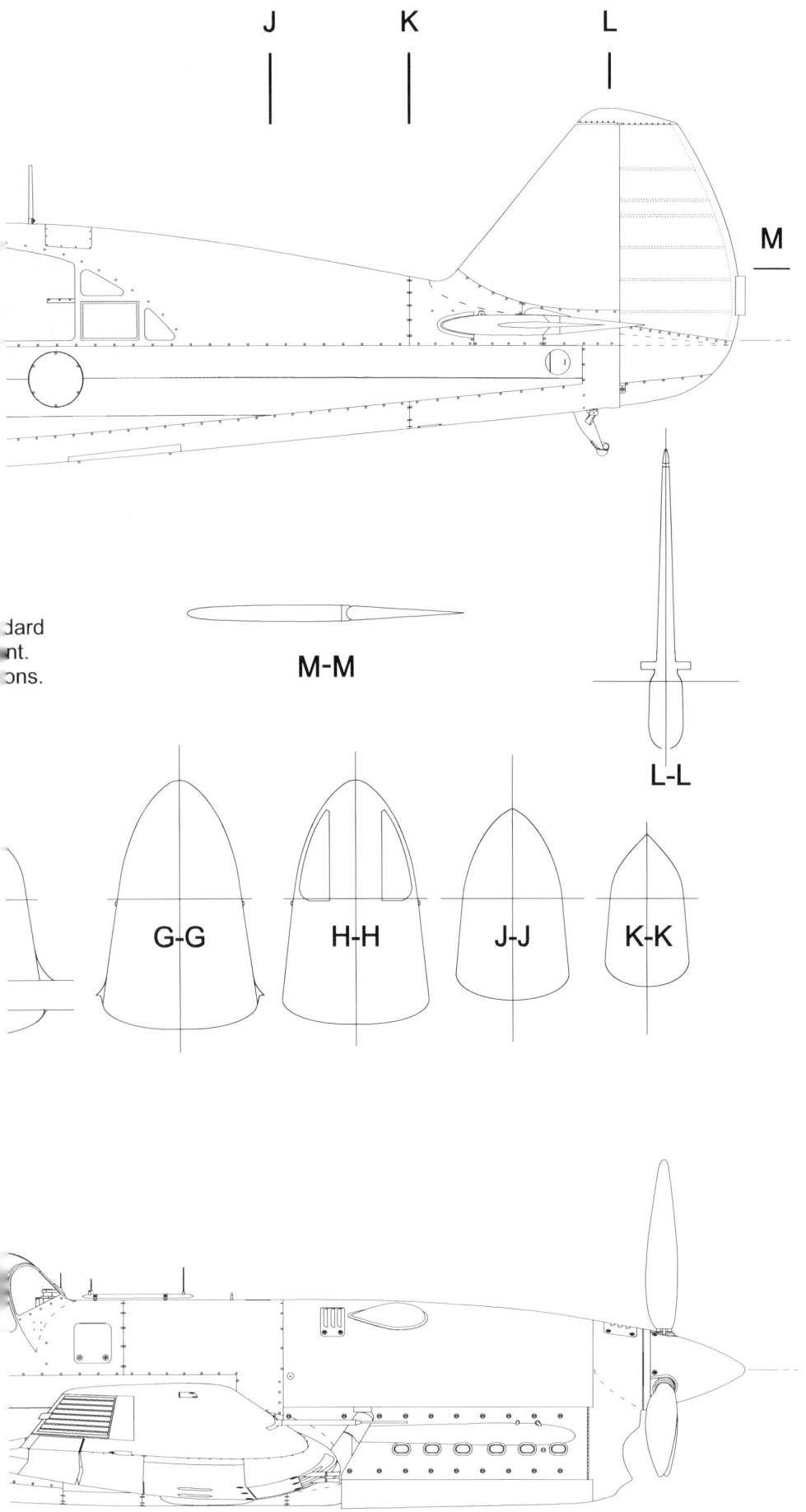

dard
nt.
ons.

M-M

L-L

G-G   H-H   J-J   K-K

7

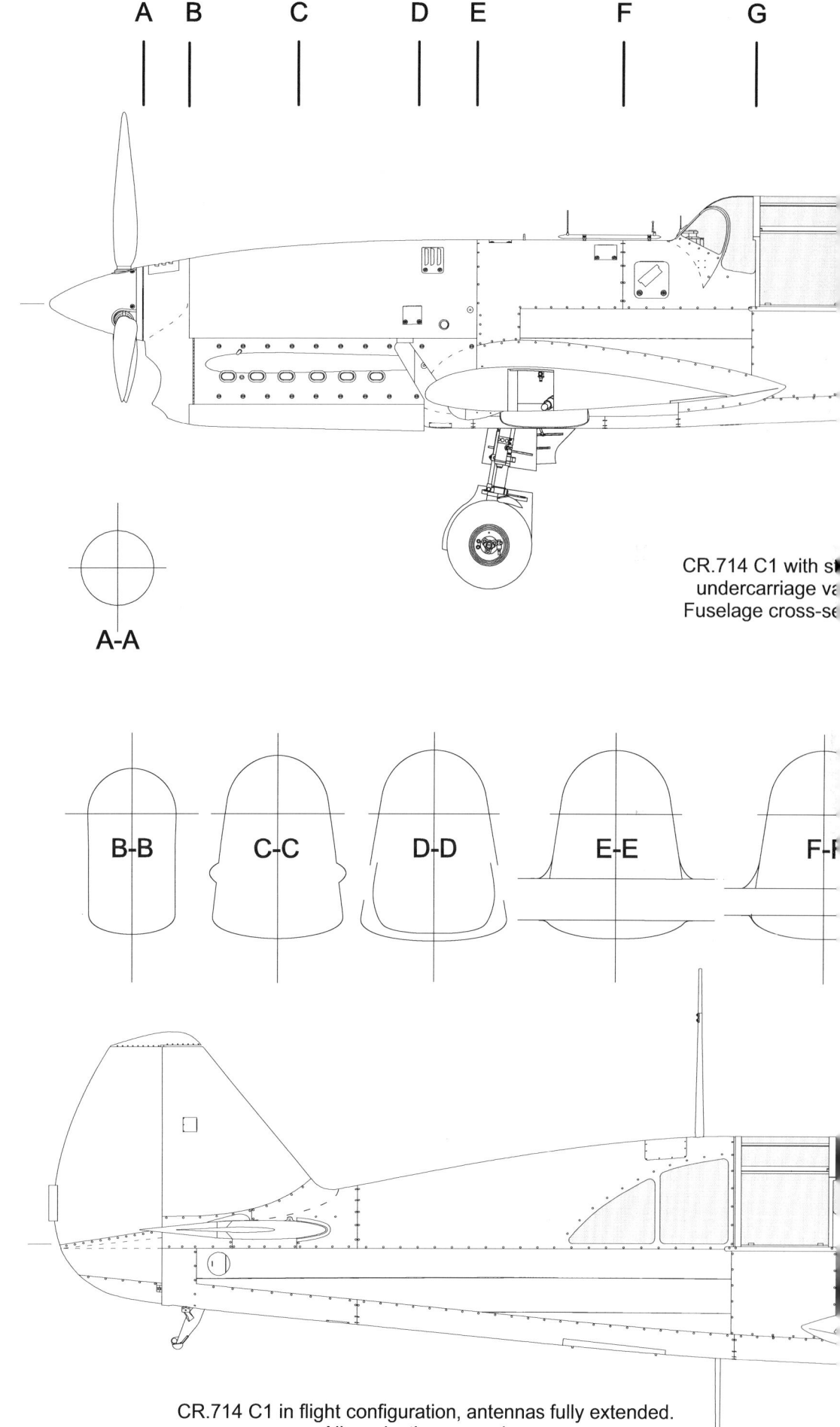

A B C D E F G

A-A

CR.714 C1 with s[...]
undercarriage va[...]
Fuselage cross-se[...]

B-B C-C D-D E-E F-[F]

CR.714 C1 in flight configuration, antennas fully extended.
All production examples.

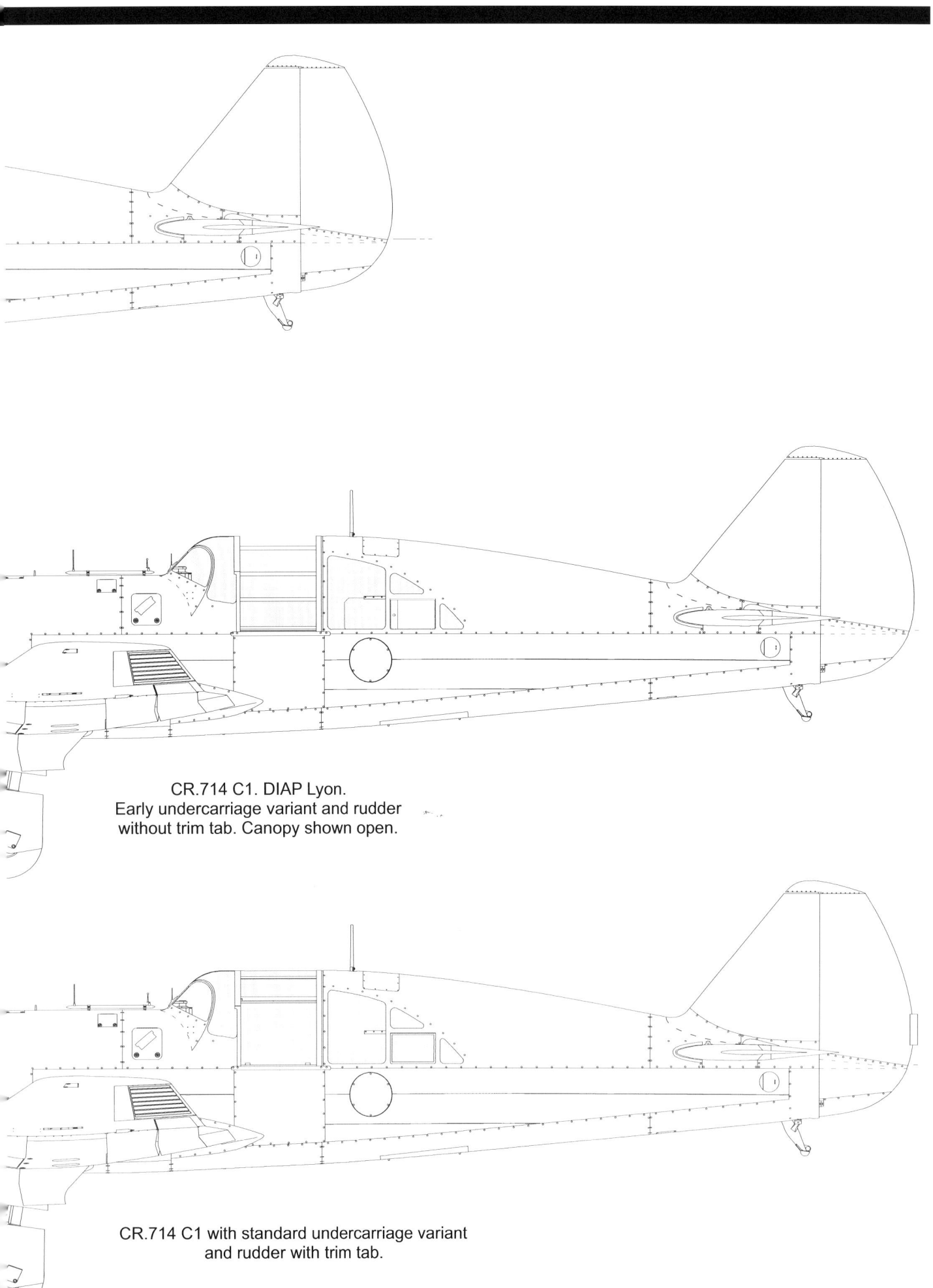

CR.714 C1. DIAP Lyon.
Early undercarriage variant and rudder
without trim tab. Canopy shown open.

CR.714 C1 with standard undercarriage variant
and rudder with trim tab.

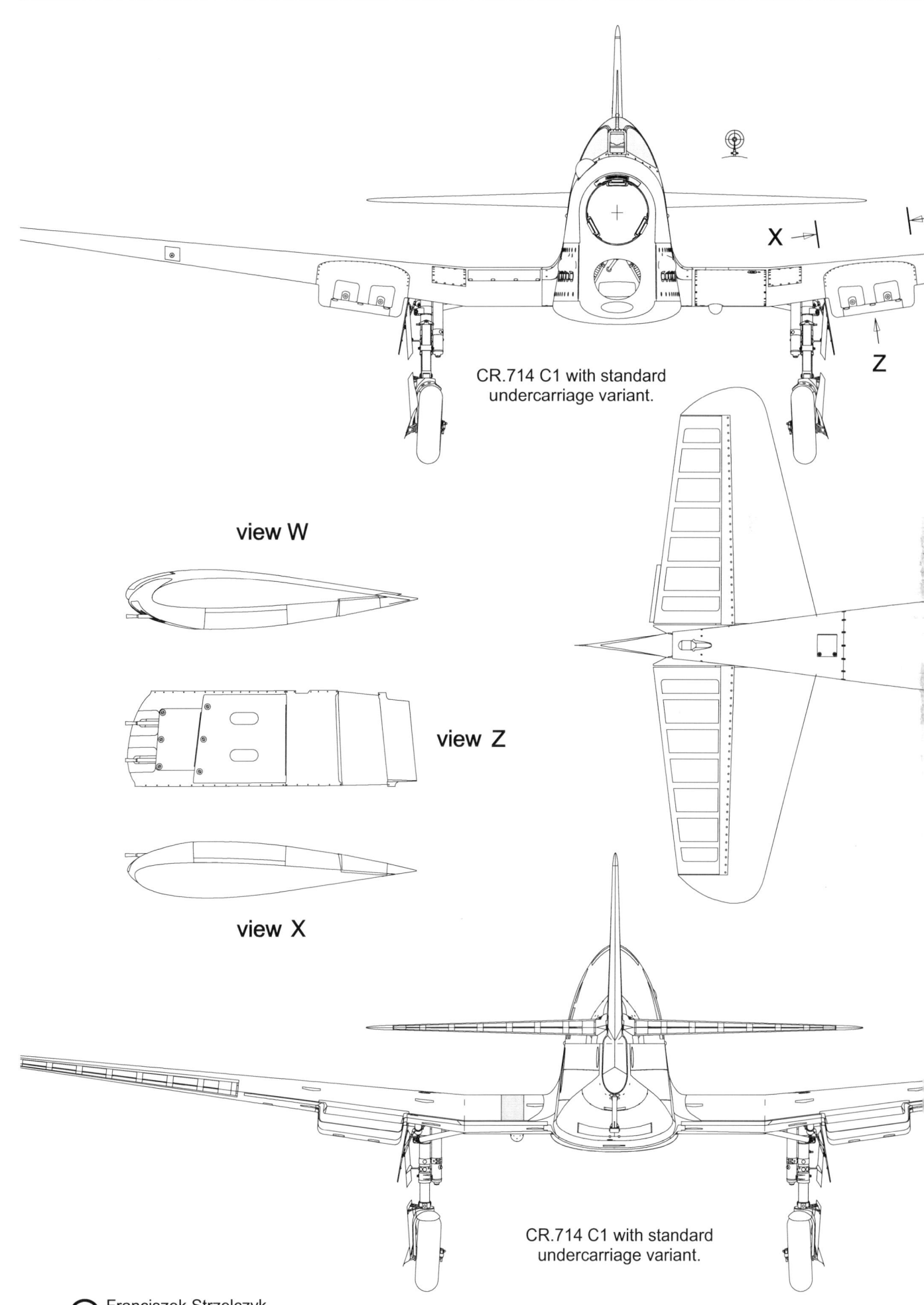

CR.714 C1 with standard
undercarriage variant.

X

Z

view W

view Z

view X

CR.714 C1 with standard
undercarriage variant.

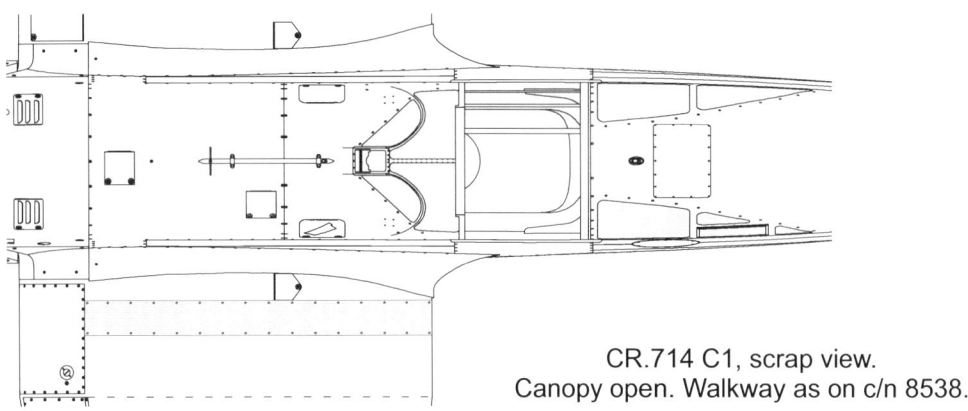

CR.714 C1, scrap view.
Canopy open. Walkway as on c/n 8538.

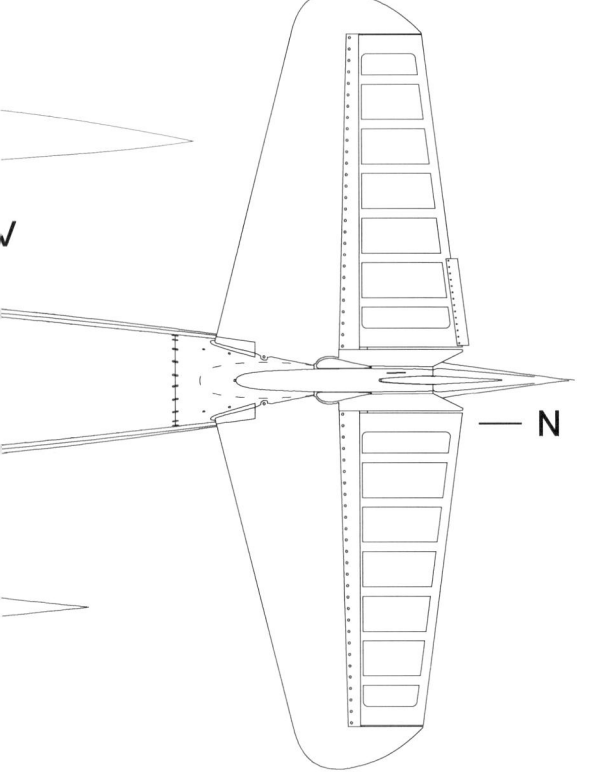

— N

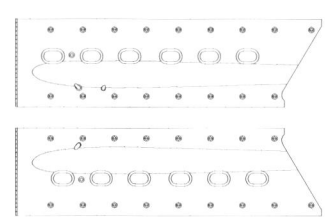

Left and right engine covers.
Note different location of openings for exhaust pipes.
All examples.

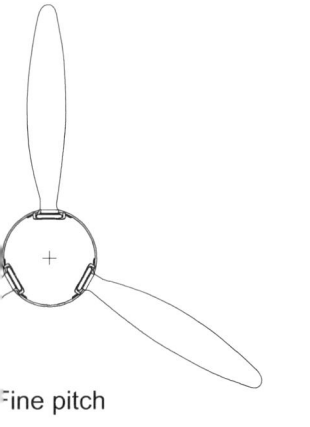

Fine pitch

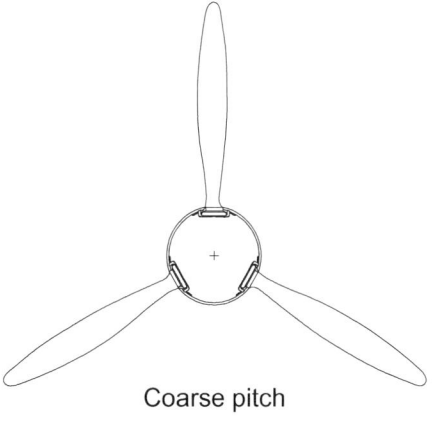

Coarse pitch

Developed
view
of blade
planform

Ratier 1644MV propeller

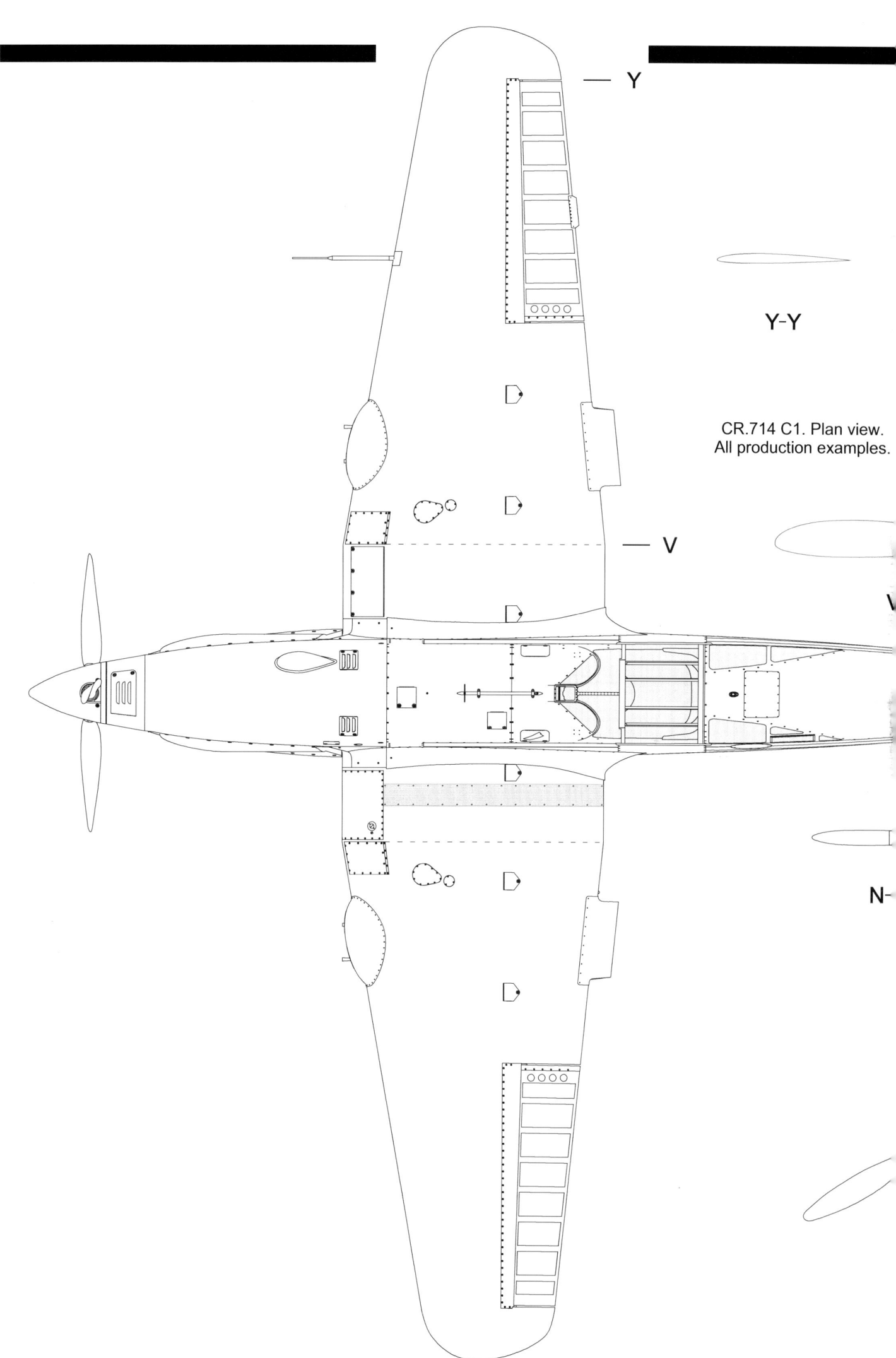

— Y

Y-Y

CR.714 C1. Plan view.
All production examples.

— V

N-

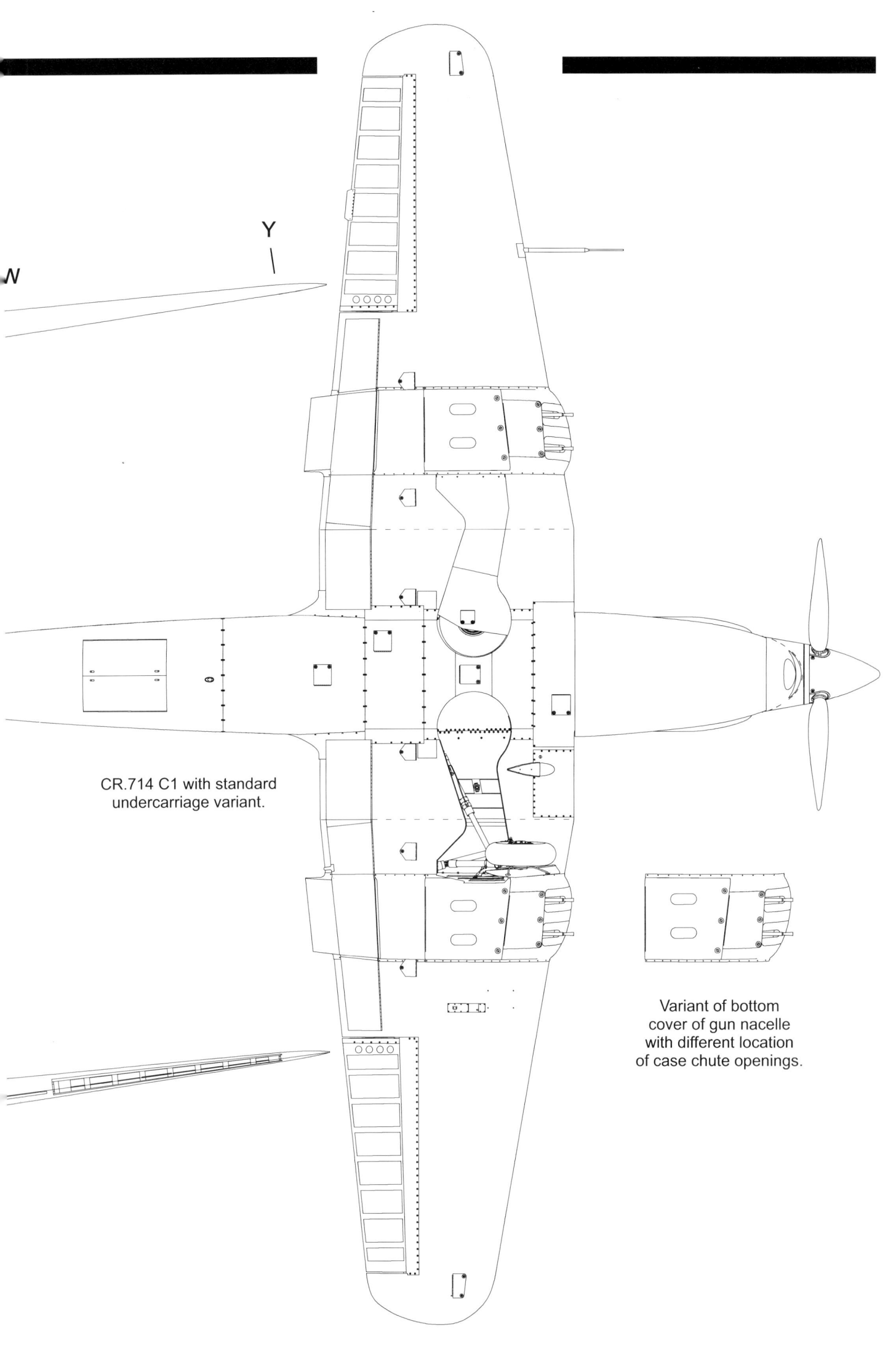

CR.714 C1 with standard
undercarriage variant.

Variant of bottom
cover of gun nacelle
with different location
of case chute openings.

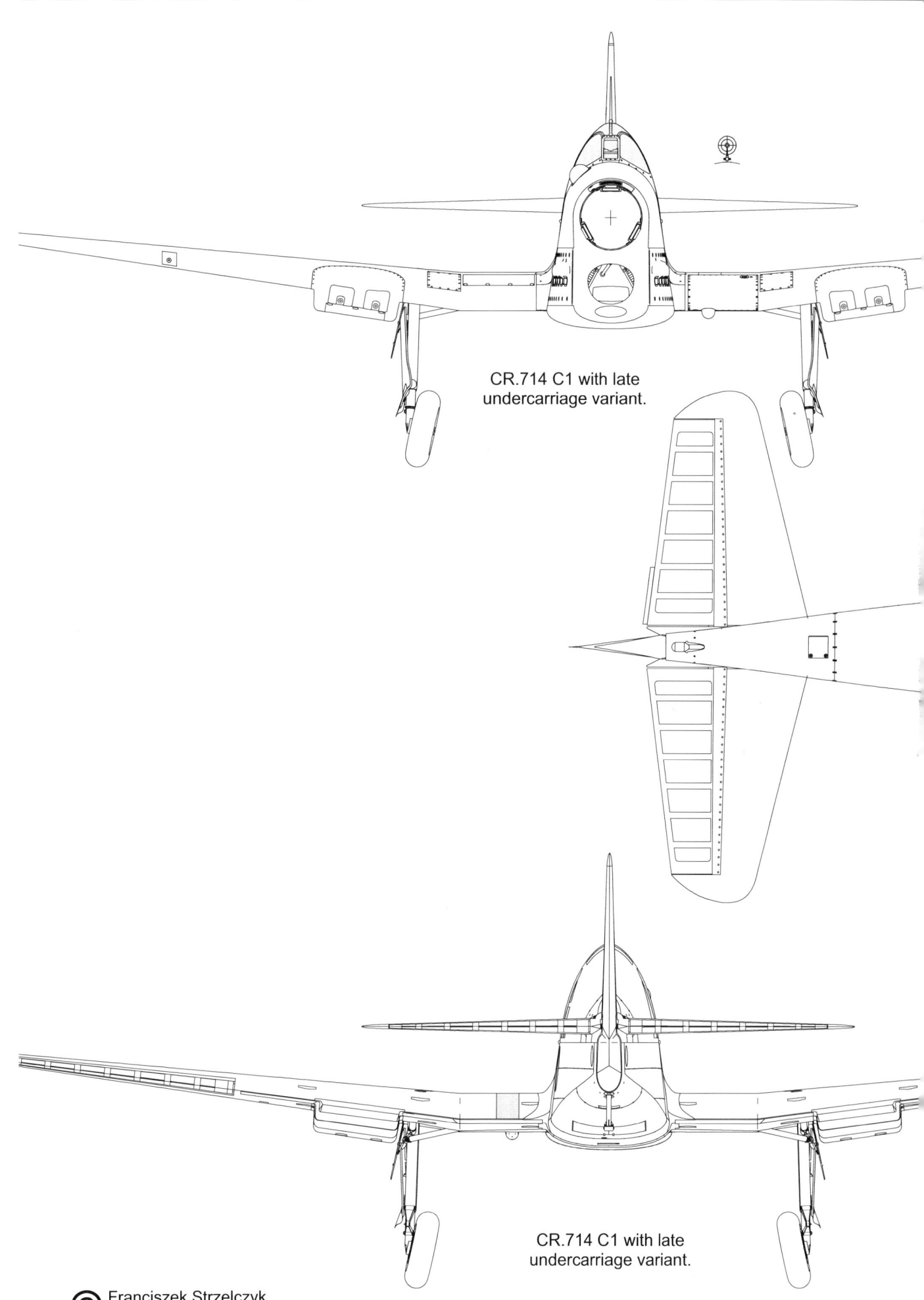

CR.714 C1 with late
undercarriage variant.

CR.714 C1 with late
undercarriage variant.

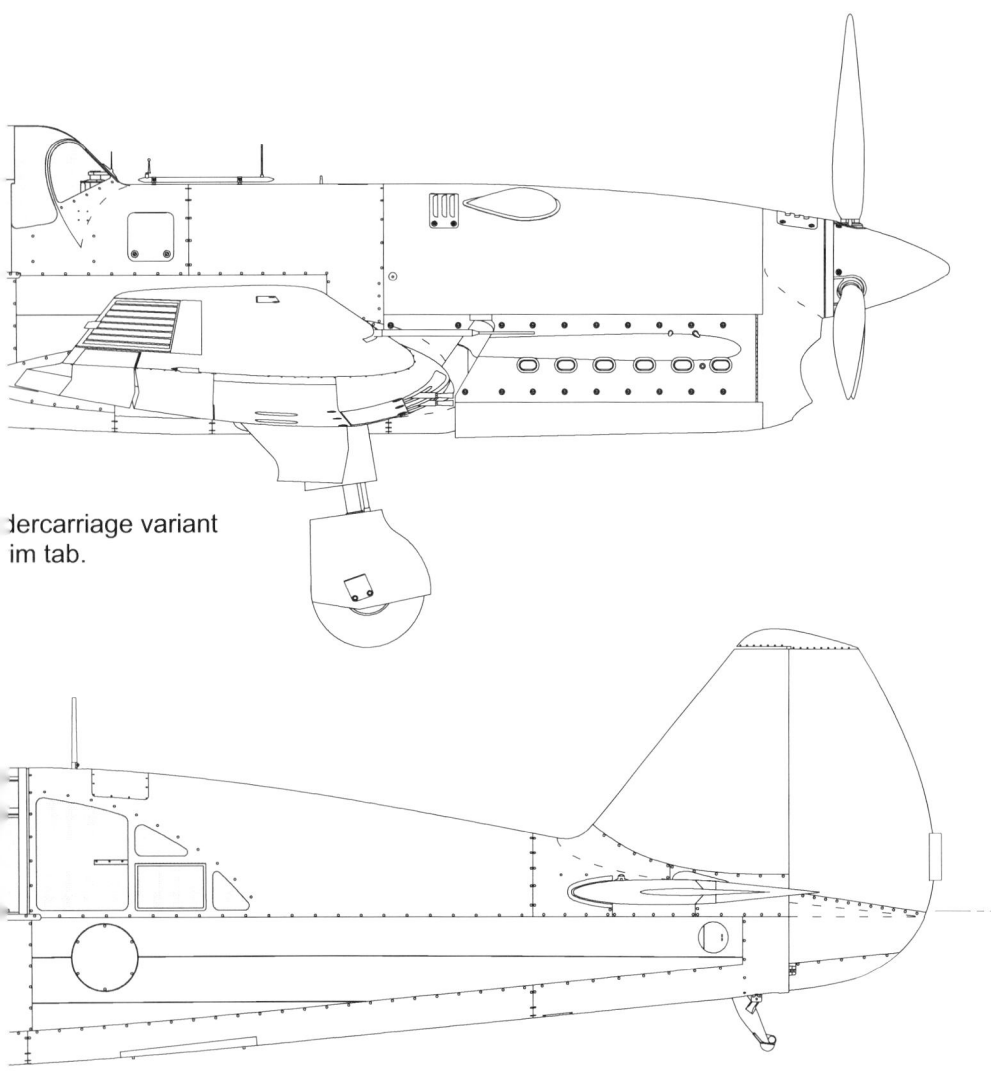

dercarriage variant
im tab.

carriage variant.

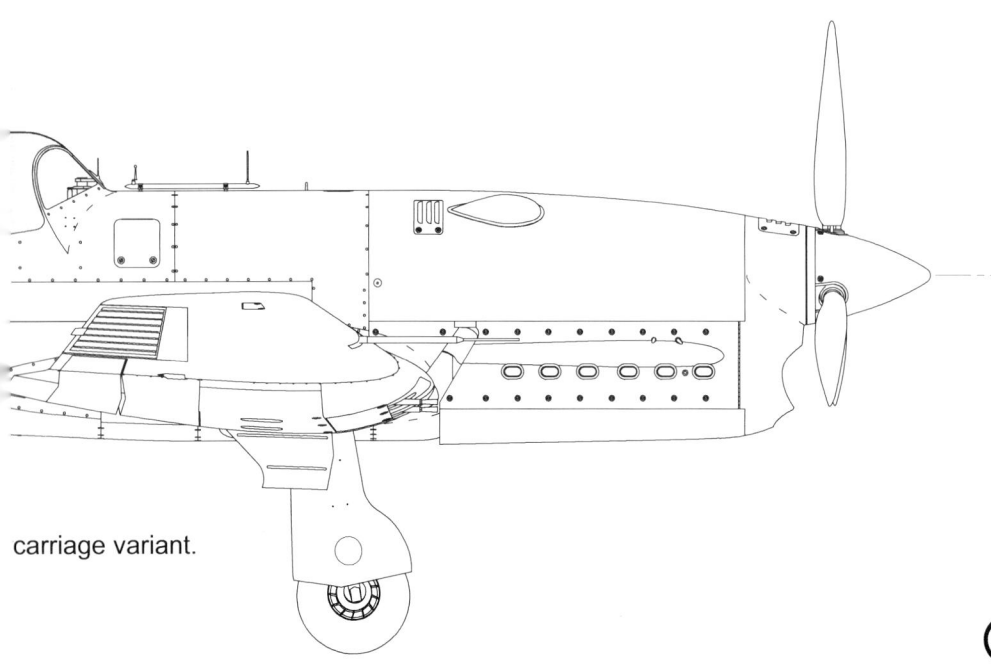

carriage variant.

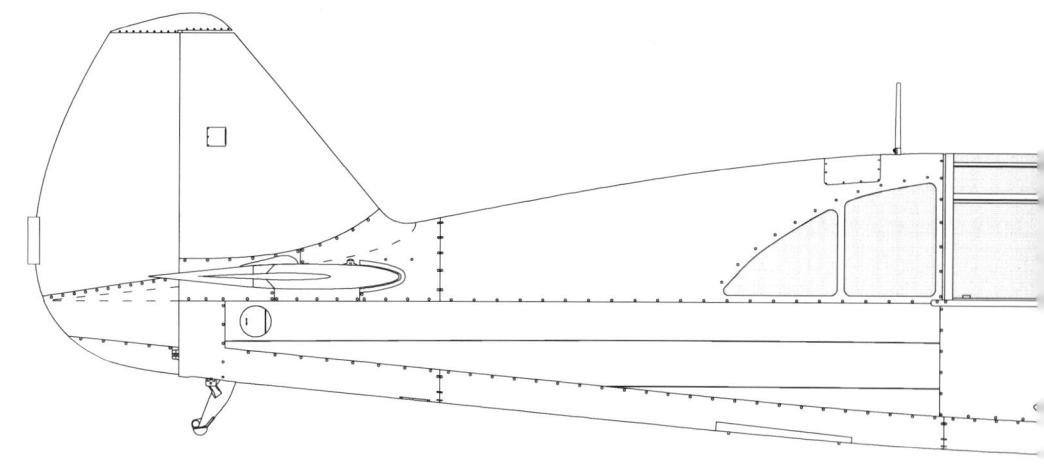

CR.714 C1 with standard
and rudder with

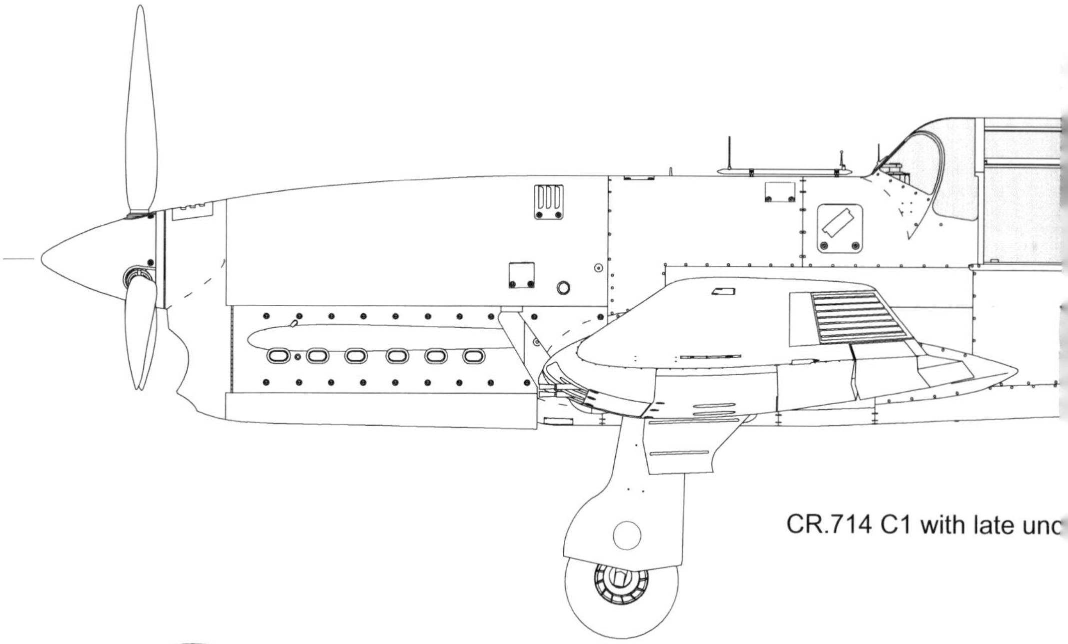

CR.714 C1 with late und

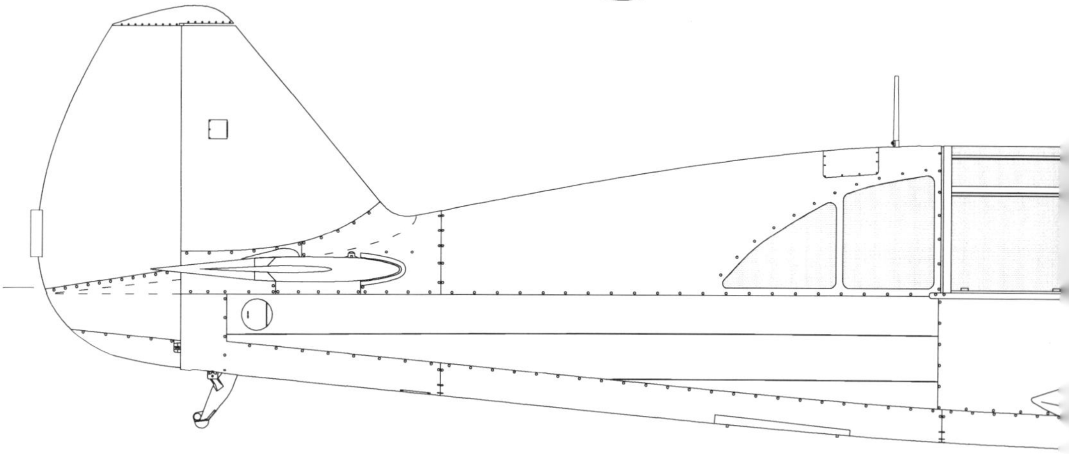

CR.714 C1 with late und

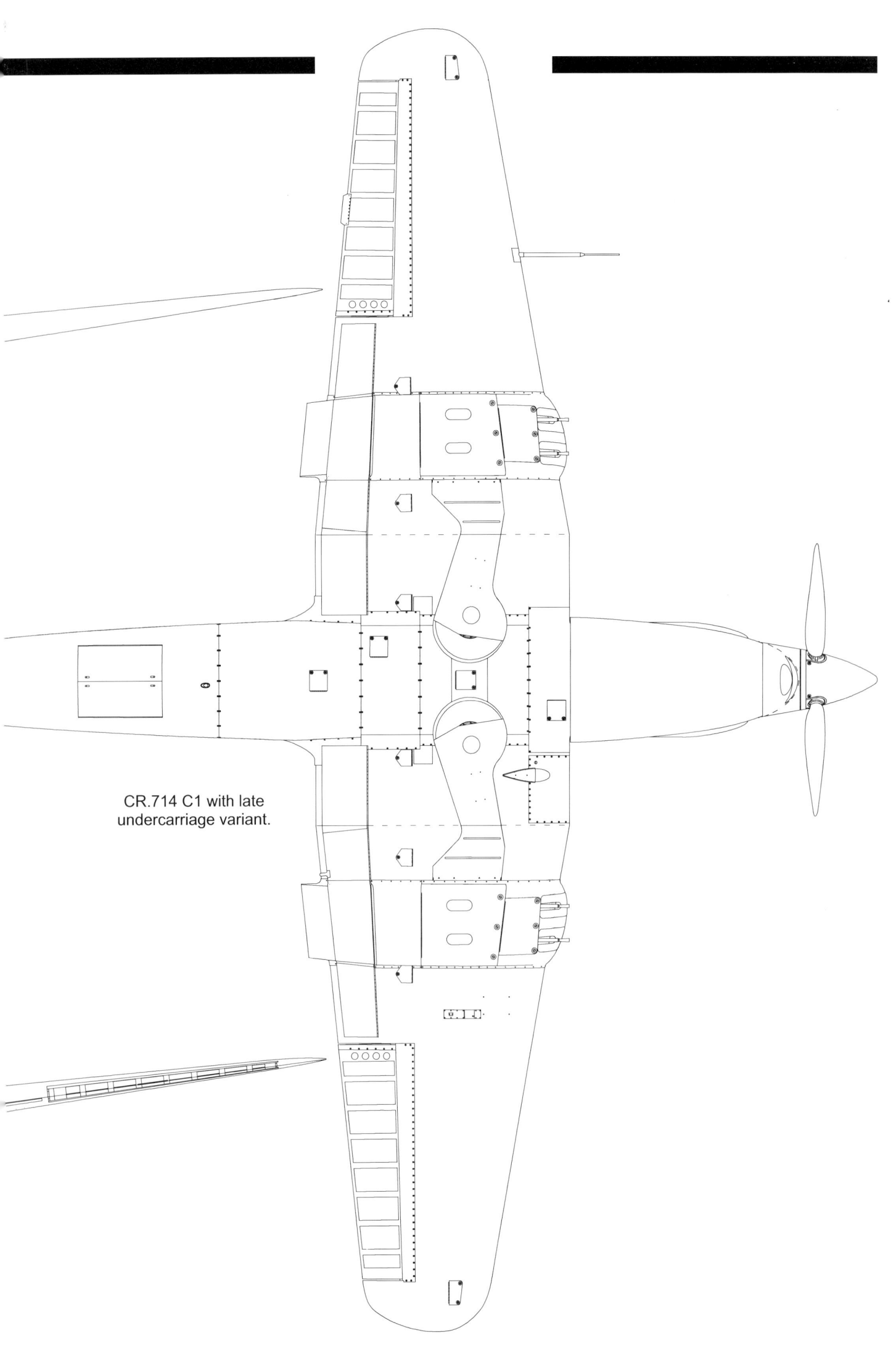

CR.714 C1 with late
undercarriage variant.